Medicine Trail

Medicine Trail

The Life and Lessons

of Gladys Tantaquidgeon

MELISSA JAYNE FAWCETT

The University of Arizona Press   Tucson

First printing

The University of Arizona Press

Manufactured in the United States of America

05 04 03 02 01 00   6 5 4 3 2 1

Library of Congress Cataloging-in-Publication Data

Fawcett, Melissa Jayne, 1960–
    Medicine trail: the life and lessons of Gladys Tantaquidgeon / Melissa
Jayne Fawcett.
        p. cm.
Includes bibliographical references.
    ISBN 0-8165-2068-2 (cloth: acid-free paper) —ISBN 0-8165-2069-0 (pbk.:
acid-free paper)
1. Tantaquidgeon, Gladys. 2. Mohegan Indians—Biography. 3. Women
shamans—Biography. 4. Mohegan Indians—Medicine. 5. Delaware
Indians—Medicine. I. Title.
    E99.M83 T364 2000
    974.7′004973–dc21
    00-008195

British Library Cataloguing-in-Publication Data

A catalogue record for this book is available from the British Library.

Publication of this book is made possible in part by the proceeds of a
permanent endowment created with the assistance of a Challenge Grant
from the National Endowment for the Humanities, a federal agency.

This book is dedicated
to the good spirits
of Mohegan Hill.

CONTENTS

ILLUSTRATIONS

page

PREFACE

The Lasting of the Mohegans

Before the night has come, have I lived to see the last warrior of the wise race of the Mohicans.

—Conclusion of *The Last of the Mohicans,* by JAMES FENIMORE COOPER

The classic novel *The Last of the Mohicans* concludes with a young Mohegan *sachem* (head chief) named Uncas jumping off a precipice to his death.[1] This story is a tragedy because he leaves behind no offspring. The real Uncas was born around 1598 and lived well into his eighties. He fathered generations of Mohegan descendants, including members of the contemporary Mohegan tribe living in Uncasville, Connecticut. Current tribal rolls list around thirteen hundred members. Most of the Mohegan children born today represent the thirteenth generation of Uncas's descendants. Because an Indian year (one full lunar cycle or rotation of the earth) includes thirteen moons, many Mohegan people believe that this thirteenth generation since Uncas brings the tribe's history full circle.

This book recounts the life of Sachem Uncas's modern-day ninth-generation granddaughter, Gladys Tantaquidgeon. Many of her grandfather Uncas's actions have echoed boldly in her lifetime. A few of his key exploits and their repercussions follow.

In 1635, Uncas was a Pequot *sagamore* (subchief) who disagreed with his sachem, Sassacus, about how to contend with the invading English. Unable to resolve their differences, Uncas broke away. He moved to Shantok on the west bank of the Thames River, where his followers declared him sachem.[2] Uncas chose to refer to his group by the tribe's old Lenni Lenape clan name Mohegan, meaning Wolf People.

x i

The new sachem pledged his friendship, along with that of his descendants, to the English, affording protection to those "pale strangers" and to his own small tribe in a tumultuous time. The Mohegans and English recognized one another's sovereignty in the Treaty of 1638. Nevertheless, as non-Indians arrived in greater numbers, they encroached upon those sovereign Mohegan lands. Following Uncas's passing, in 1682 or 1683, his nation stumbled.[3]

When the Connecticut colony became a state after the American Revolution, the Mohegans avoided a federal relationship because early United States Indian policy seemed to be predicated on warfare with native nations. During the nineteenth century, the state of Connecticut and the Mohegans remained mutually tolerant, due to their friendly colonial relations. As a result, the Mohegans had no need for federal recognition for quite some time.

By the twentieth century, however, nearly all indigenous entitlements had become the responsibility of the U.S. government. Consequently, in 1978, when Congress created a new Native American recognition process, the Mohegans submitted their application. Formal acknowledgment of sovereignty required that the tribe prove its social and political continuity since European contact.

Throughout those centuries since first encountering the non-Indian, Mohegans had maintained their land base and traditions. The U.S. government, after reviewing more than twenty thousand pages of documents, legally affirmed the sovereign status of the Mohegan Nation in March 1994.

Mohegan tribal government today is surprisingly similar to that of Uncas's day. The nine-member Tribal Council still holds legislative and executive powers, just as it did when Uncas conducted meetings atop Cochegun Rock four centuries ago. The Council of Elders continues to perform cultural and judicial functions, including bestowal of traditional titles, such as chief, medicine woman, fire keeper, and pipe carrier. Other Mohegan customs carried forth from that ancient era include respect for the tribe's matriarchal practices, reverence for tribal elders, and maintenance of Uncas's friendship with the non-Indian.

The contemporary Mohegan Indian Reservation includes the old territory of Shantok and the adjacent environs beside the Thames River. Settlers named the town bordering the reservation Montville, but everyone still refers to the area surrounding the reservation as Uncasville.

Much credit for tribal survival is due to Uncas's decisions and those of the chiefs and tribespeople after him who followed his example. The tribe must also acknowledge a continuous line of women faith keepers for its endurance. Among them is the present medicine woman, Dr. Gladys Iola Tantaquidgeon. Gladys holds honorary doctoral degrees from the University of Connecticut and Yale. She has also received many awards and honors, including admission to the Connecticut Women's Hall of Fame. A life-size painted statue of her, carved in sacred basswood, graces the Mohegan reservation. Tribal members refer to it simply as Gladys, a name that (like Uncas's) commands the respect of all Mohegans past, present, and future.

ACKNOWLEDGMENTS

I recorded this text by listening to Gladys Tantaquidgeon over a lifetime and occasionally taping or taking notes on her words. All quotations not footnoted are from my taped recordings, written notes, and recollections. This book is not an academic research monograph. Neither is it a contemporary-style oral history based on taped interviews conducted by an outsider or professional for the purpose of creating a linear evaluation of a person or group. Rather, it is a life story told from the collective perspective of an indigenous nation. In Mohegan oral tradition, the life of any one leader is inseparable from the story of the people as a whole. Gladys Tantaquidgeon's biography epitomizes that seamlessness. Chosen to perform a traditional function, Gladys is an extraordinary being who became an archetype of Mohegan culture.

Mohegan oral tradition also requires that we internalize its lessons in order to complete the process of transmitting cultural information. We ritualize words, phrases, and beliefs about people, places, events, and spirit beings as they pass from one generation to the next. This method of cultural transmission promotes deep understanding. My great-uncle, Chief Harold Tantaquidgeon, taught me, "If you can forget it, you never really knew it."

In 1940, Gladys scribed her own majestic view of our enduring oral tradition in her personal papers.

What would the Old World historic shrines and scenes be without their traditions and classical associations? And what would the New World scenes be without their human traditions recited as the ancients knew them to lift our imaginations above the land and sea into the clouds? But where are the spokesmen for the age of legend of the natives? Who is to tell us now that the [east] coast [was] the central scene of an epic, a national legend. . . . What link have we with the past . . . to help us conjure up the sagas of sea and islands, of heroes, of whales, of shoals, dunes, and forests coming and going as the heroes will it? . . . Ponder upon the wonder that has happened to preserve the sagas of beautiful regions redeemed at the last moment and enjoy it. It is almost a miracle for the literature of the land!

The reader may attribute interpretations within this book to the wisdom of Gladys coupled with the insights of many Indians throughout the eastern woodlands. As shown above, I have framed Gladys's own writings and words in order to highlight them.

The inspiration for this book came largely from Gladys. Nevertheless, no truly Indian story comes from any one or two authors or even the members of any single generation or tribe. The following Indian traditionalists shared many insights herein: Trudie Richmond (Schaghticoke), Ella Sekatau and John Brown (Narragansetts), Joseph Bruchac and Donna Roberts (Abenakis), and Jayne Fawcett, Ruth Tantaquidgeon, Anita Fowler, Courtland Fowler, Kathy Bernier, Stacy Dufresne, Sandra Eichelberg, and Sandi Pineault (Mohegans). I thank these individuals for their offerings of good spirits and send them many prayers of gratitude. I must also profoundly thank Gunci Mundo, the Great Spirit, for giving me the privilege of spending so much of my young life in the company of Gladys Tantaquidgeon. Great thanks is also due the *Makiawisug,* "Little People of the Woodlands," for the many blessings they continue to bestow upon me and all others who believe.

Mundo Wigo, "The Creator is good."

Medicine Trail

CHAPTER 1

INTRODUCTION TO THE TRAIL OF LIFE

We walk as a single spirit on the Trail of Life.

—from the Mohegan Vision Statement, 1997

The Mohegan Trail of Life is as old as memory. In each generation, elders pass on the knowledge of its ancient design to the Mohegan Indian people. Gladys Tantaquidgeon is the tribe's hundred-year-old medicine woman, and her life story reflects the essence of the trail's spirit and meaning.

The Trail of Life pattern decorates her ceremonial regalia because life's journey is itself a circle. Her ancestors painted it onto baskets, the oldest that she cares for at her museum, because Mohegans record their life trails on their handiwork. There are many ups and downs in the trail design, reflecting the rolling hills of New England and the bumpy challenges of life itself. Dots beside the trail signify people met along life's journey; leaves symbolize the healing medicine plants of the eastern woodlands.

Mohegan Vision Statement

We are the Wolf People, children of Mundo, a part of the Tree of Life.
Our ancestors form our roots, our living Tribe is the trunk, our
    grandchildren are the buds of our future.
We remember and teach the stories of our ancestors.
We watch. We listen. We learn.
We respect Mother Earth, our Elders, and all that comes from Mundo.
We are willing to break arrows of peace to heal old and new wounds.
We acknowledge and learn from our mistakes.

3

> We walk as a single spirit on the Trail of Life.
> We are guided by thirteen generations past and responsible to
>   thirteen generations to come.
> We survive as a nation guided by the wisdom of our past.
> Our circular trail returns us to wholeness as a people. *Ni Ya Yo,* "It Is
>   So"
>
> —Adopted by a consensus of the Mohegan Council of Elders in 1997

Gladys teaches that we also call this trail the Path of the Sun, for it follows life's circle from birth and sunrise (in the east) to death and passage into the spirit world (in the west)—then on again to rebirth and the dawn of the next generation. Gizaxk (Father Sun) and Doyup (Grandfather Turtle) oversee this journey. When Father Sun rises and sets each day, he travels over and under the rounded back of Grandfather Turtle. Atop the turtle's back, the Creator formed this earth. In the story that follows, Gladys's travels mirror Father Sun's eternal path by beginning in the east, moving west, then going back east again.

The Lenni Lenape (Delaware) medicine man Witaponoxwe (Walks with Daylight) gave Gladys yet another understanding of the Trail of Life or Path of the Sun symbol. His Lenape people were ancient ancestors of the Mohegan who used that design to depict the journey of the spirit after death. They called that ultimate trek the Beautiful White Path. Ceremonial pipe smoke follows that Beautiful Path as it enters the blackness of the cosmos. Once it has left the earthly realm, smoke travels to the Smokey Way (known as the Milky Way to non-Indian people), where it sends terrestrial messages to the great celestial beings who live amid that star-way.

In that deeper way of knowing, the tiny white beads on black velvet (along the trail on Gladys's regalia collar) depict both people and stars in the dark of night. Stars are the advanced form taken by Indian people with extraordinary gifts of the spirit after they pass into the spirit world.[4] The Beautiful White Path, Trail of Life, and Path of the Sun are all portions of one journey. Each represents part of a singular circular trail, traveled in three states of being—the celestial-being form, the earth-life form, and the spirit form.

Gladys (wearing Winnebago appliqué shirt) beside her regalia at Tantaquidgeon Museum, circa 1985. The eighteenth-century belt belonged to Fidelia Fielding and Martha Uncas. The collar features the Trail of Life design.

The following account recalls Gladys Tantaquidgeon's Trail of Life here on earth. It records one portion of her three-part trek that foreshadows the other two. Journey now from east to west and back again, along the ups and downs of the twinkling life trail that will one day include Gladys Tantaquidgeon's star.

~~~~~

PART I

MOHEGAN HILL TRAIL

CHAPTER 2

FOLKS ON THE HILL

The eagle hath its place of rest,
The wild horse where to dwell,
And the spirit that gave the bird its nest
Made me a home as well.
—from "The Indian Hunter Song"

To the unknowing, Mohegan Hill appears as a simple mound on the Route 32 highway in southeastern Connecticut. A first glance reveals only modest houses and a meager landscape of oak and maple sprinkled with pine and cedar atop unworkable, rocky soil. Yet Mohegan people have fought to maintain this hill as their home for centuries. Every nation has a spirit, and Mohegan Hill is the special place where Mohegan spirit looms large. Mohegans are not simply tied to the hill. They are of it. Gentle spirits protect those who live here. In each generation, some serve as its chosen caretakers. For the twentieth century, Gladys Tantaquidgeon has been that special guardian. She alone hears the secret whispers of all the beings who reside there.

Gladys entered this magical hilltop world on June 15, 1899, just in time to greet the final summer solstice of the nineteenth century. Like the medicine women before her, she found her most respected teachers in the plants, animals, spirits, and people of the hill. From them, she learned the mundane, magical, and mysterious lessons of the place called Mohegan.

Her mother was expert at beading, quilting, and sewing. She was a traditionalist and raised Gladys according to ancient guidelines. Harriet Tantaquidgeon bit her daughter's fingernails, never clipped them, until Gladys's first birthday, to prevent her from ever becoming a thief. Gladys's hair was trimmed when the moon was waning to ensure thickness, health, and shine. Her mother turned over Gladys's shoes at night to prevent bad dreams. She kept her daughter's lost teeth away from animals who could invoke charms to make them large and crooked. She frightened away coughs with a pungent onion poultice. Most important, she put Gladys to bed each night before the whippoorwill called. Early rest prevented capture by the Makiawisug—those mischievous Little People of the Woodlands who gather stray Mohegan children to live with them underground. Harriet raised all of her children in this old way.

My parents had ten children. Three died in infancy, and I didn't know them. Of the remaining seven, there was one brother and one sister older. I was the older of the younger five children—two brothers and two sisters. The surviving were Burrill, who was older, then Lillian, then I came along. Then there was Earl, he died about the age of twenty, then Harold, then Winifred, then Ruth.

Gladys's father, John, also came from a very conservative Mohegan Indian family. Though his parents passed away when he was young, his cousin Jerome Bohema trained him in the old ways of the woods. John planted a cedar tree to commemorate Gladys's birth and recorded her growth by making notches in an upright of his woodpile. He taught her to gather basket splints from only the north side of the hill where they were sturdy. Gladys learned to gauge their width by eye and make a proper handle that hitched when picked up. To chart underground water, he showed her the art of divining with forked sticks made of witch hazel, wild plum, or wild apple.

Harriet and John were rock-solid Indians, embedded like stones in the hill. They handled Gladys's daily upbringing. Meanwhile, tribal elders, like Medicine Woman Emma Baker and Faith Keeper Fidelia Fielding, gave her knowledge of the ways of the spirit that are not of this world. Together, all the Indians of the hill taught Gladys to love and laugh her way through adversity. They checked her ego with expressions such as "You don't know beans when the bag's untied" and "Who died and left you in charge?" The way of the hill folk brought joy, stability, and good medicine to Gladys's youth. The white man's attempts to take away the customs of the folks on the hill seemed only to make their good spirits stronger.

Hundreds of well-worn trails crisscrossed Mohegan Hill, interconnecting the hill folk. Pathways led from Mohegan Church to the Muggs Hole beside Gladys's home on Church Lane, over the top of Uncas Hill to the parsonage, from the Shantok burial ground to all the houses on the hilltop, from the base of Fort Hill past the remains of Chief Uncas's old stone fort (on its summit) over to Stony Brook, and from the Little House north through Massapeag.

Central to these well-worn trails was the Tantaquidgeon home—a rambling, cedar-shingled house known as the Fielding homestead. There, after she reached eight years of age, old folks taught Gladys to sew rickrack borders onto calico dresses. She learned to design woolen coats for her family; her sister Ruth's favorite was a red one with white fur trim. Her artful hands beaded dark velvet "puzzle pouches" and pincushions. She made jewel-toned fabric scraps into crazy quilts and sorted yarn by colors for finger weaving. Her first lessons in cooking included traditional yellow-eye baked beans roasted overnight with honey, ketchup, mustard, brown sugar, onion, and salt pork. The Tantaquidgeons always served them with fried doughboys on Saturday nights. Sunday dinners, held at noontime, drew friends and family. By the time she was a teenager, Gladys welcomed those crowds with her own version of "soup on the hill"—an all-around favorite made of rutabaga, carrots, potatoes, celery, and onion, seasoned just right, and simmered into stock with a chunk of meat.

That old Fielding homestead hosted generations of Mohegan spirits representing earthly residents of years past. Those spirits included Rachel Fielding, who sent a dream-message to her daughter, Medicine Woman Emma Baker, to restore the tribe's ancient Wigwam festival at Mohegan Church. While tribespeople were constructing Mohegan Church in the early 1830s, Rachel Fielding's homestead had served as a temporary church and school. The church had been founded with the support of Rachel's mother, Cynthia Teecomwas Hoscott, her grandmother, Lucy Tantaquidgeon Teecomwas, and her great-grandmother, Great Lucy Occum Tantaquidgeon.

Those four generations of Mohegan women lived together and fought hard for the creation of that structure. Its purpose was to prevent Mohegans from being relocated, for by the 1830s, federal law required any unschooled or nonchurchgoing Indians to go West; it had forced the Cherokee to march on their Trail of Tears.

When Gladys was a child, church hymn-sings drew several dozen folks from the hill and featured songs like "Let the Lower Lights Be Burning," "Shall We Gather at the River," and "Rescue the Perishing." Amateur nights were fashionable, as were plays such as "The Old Peabody Pew." Also popular were thirty-five-cent escalloped oyster suppers held under the trees, topped off by Martha Washington pie.

The church was not only a social hub but also a constant reminder of that dangerous era when the U.S. government wanted Mohegans removed from the hill. Cautionary tales of those times encouraged Gladys to scrutinize the motives of her non-Indian schooling and to cherish the lessons taught to her at home. The lyrics of "The Indian Hunter Song" sung to Gladys as a child by her grandfather Eliphalet Peegee Fielding was just such a warning:

> Oh, why does the white man follow my path
> Like the hounds on the tiger's track?
> Does the flush on my dark cheek
> Waken his wrath?
> Does he court the bow at my back?

He has rivers and seas where the billows and breeze
Bear riches for him alone;
And the sons of the wood never
Plunge in the flood
Which the white man called his own.
Then why should he come to the
Streams where none but the red skin dare to swim?
Why, why should he wrong the
Hunter, one who never did harm to him?
Wha—Wha—Wha—Wha

The father above thought fit to give
The white man corn and wine;
There is gold in fields where they may live,
But the forest shades are mine.
The eagle hath its place of rest,
The wild horse where to dwell,
And the spirit that gave the bird its nest
Made me a home as well.
Go back, go back from the red man's track
For the hunter's eyes grow dim,
To find that the white man wrongs the one
Who never did harm to him.
Wha—Wha—Wha—Wha[5]

Primarily educated at home by her elders, Gladys infrequently attended the non-Indian grammar school at the foot of Mohegan Hill. At one point, her parents moved to New London, hoping that she might receive a better education. However, Gladys never went to high school and, apparently, did not need to, since she eventually enrolled in college. Her memories of grade school are sketchy, unlike her vivid recollections of the old homestead where she received her elders' teachings.

Before I moved to New London, I liked history. But I had trouble with dates. They were kind of scared out of me. In the "numbers classes" I probably

Mohegan School at the foot of Mohegan Hill, circa 1906. Gladys, at age seven, is third from the left, second row.

didn't do too well. My maternal grandmother taught me most of what I learned. I don't recall if I had any books or not.

When my parents moved to New London, I attended Robert Bartlett School and then went to Nathan Hale Grammar School. Then I entered third grade, and we were probably in New London seven years. So I attended grade school there. There were not any other Indian children in New London.

We lived in New London for a time, then moved back to Mohegan, to the old homestead. It had once been the home of Cynthia Teecomwas Hoscott and her daughter, Rachel Hoscott Fielding.

It was an old farmhouse with the old boards on the floor, two fireplaces, and another section had been built onto the original building. A narrow stairway led to two bedrooms upstairs and two downstairs and a huge kitchen.

The two sections of the house both had a parlor, but we didn't go into those rooms very often.

We had woodstoves, and we had to put butter and milk down the well in containers to keep cool—and that was not far from the back door. My uncle Ned Fowler and Nettie, his wife, lived in the section built on, and I spent a great deal of time with my Uncle Ned. Father was a stonemason and carpenter, and mother was busy with children. Aunt Nettie, a practical nurse, and Grandmother Fielding cooked and kept house in the section with Uncle Ned. He had a garden three-quarters of a mile away, and sometimes I wanted to go with him. For a while, as a child, I raised chickens.

I didn't have any high school training, and what I learned in between times was more or less on my own.

Gladys's great-aunt Emma Baker led the Church Ladies Sewing Society meetings, where the members considered potential new chiefs, discussed land claims, and evaluated promising children. The tribe's ancient matriarchy had chosen this group as their new venue. When they gathered, these women crafted not only tribal society and politics but also eloquent handiwork to sell at the annual Wigwam. Meanwhile, Mohegan men carved stone and wooden items destined to grace some of the finest museums in the world. Gladys's father, John, was one of the best artisans, using "crooked knives," thin, curved blades, to carve sweet maple into wooden scoops, spoons, and bowls decorated with woodland leaves and cornflowers. He also wove the tightest ash and oak splint baskets in southern New England. Roscoe Skeesucks was one of the few who surpassed him in skill. He was a Nehantic-Mohegan man whose name meant Little Eyes. Ross was particularly famous for his carvings of owl-handled ladles and turtle-head "puddin' sticks," cooking utensils that resembled the old paddles that teachers hung on the wall. Gladys's uncle, Chief Matahga, knew the power of carving spirit faces onto utensils and animals onto war clubs. Her brother Harold fashioned stone pipes with an X to symbolize the four directions surrounded by four people-dots (representing his esteemed ancestors: Uncas, Sassacus, Occum, and Tantaquidgeon). As they worked, these men spoke of the meaning behind the designs in their work and of the ceremonies related to them.

From 1899 to 1912, Gladys was cocooned in good spirits and great craftsmanship. The old folks taught her fine artistic techniques, along with good medicine, which is their necessary corollary. They maintained her positive attitude and cultivated her artistic talents with good times on the hill— good food, good music, and good mischief.

Father was a very quiet man, and mother was outgoing and very popular with all the nieces and nephews. People liked to come to our home. Father played the violin, and mother played piano. Everybody would gather round and have a hymn-sing. There were "watch nights," where everyone stayed up past midnight, and "pound parties," and if you were going to them, you would take a pound of sugar, a pound of butter, a pound of flour, and so on. They go from house to house. Sometimes it might be a big surprise. Sometimes in cold, stormy weather, they came in their sleighs. It would be about every two weeks until 1918 or 1920. There were amateur nights at the church. Nanu Fowler had a bake shop, and Ed Fowler had a dance pavilion. Mother played piano, and father, violin. On Saturday nights at Sussman Hall, the dancing was led by the one-eyed prompter Tommy Wilbur. . . .

There was also square dancing. Sometimes the men dressed up as women at the square dances. One time, one of these "women" asked for a place to stay. The Mohegan women thought this strange woman seemed to be paying too much attention to the men.

While the older Mohegan women took up much of Gladys's time educating her in traditional tribal ways, she found balance in the entertaining stories of the men. Uncle Ed Fowler taught her about old-time whaling days when Mohegans hunted the great *powdawes* (whales) in dugout canoes with bone harpoons on Long Island Sound. He told her that dogwood blossoms heralded the shad-fishing season and that digging crabs when the moon was full was best. Her father, John, named for Old Man John Tantaquidgeon, shared stories about that soldier in the American Revolutionary War who sailed aboard the privateer named *Putnam*. Old Man Tantaquidgeon lived more than a century and used to say, "I fought for you, and I fought for my country." Like him a man of the sea, John could pull up steamer clams with his feet and gather the best scallops in the world from Niantic Bay. There was an unbroken connection between Mohegan men and the local waterways of the Thames River and nearby Long Island Sound. Staples of Tantaquidgeon family dinners were fried mackerel, codfish, oyster stew, and lots of clam chowder. None of the Tantaquidgeon sisters learned how to swim. Instead, they enjoyed the river for skating parties, and when its ice was extra thick, they joined sleigh races along its course.

The men told many cautionary tales about dangerous places along the river, among them Sandy Desert, Hobbomocko's Hollow, and the Shumway house. At Sandy Desert, an ancient curse had resulted in a terrible plague, making that area forbidden. The story was that the Mohegans had once given a group of fleeing Indians permission to live there. However, one day, a Mohegan runner found all those refugees suddenly dead. Not even vegetation grew in that place after that time.

Near Sandy Desert was the spooky house of Jeremiah Shumway. John Tantaquidgeon had been Shumway's ward until his mysterious disappearance in the 1870s. Local police discovered that a farmer named Gallivan had murdered Shumway and fed his diced-up remains to hogs, which he sold to a nearby butcher. Folks used to say that "there was a little Shumway in all of us"! That gruesome incident declared the Shumway house off-limits as well. The people of the hill consciously avoided such bad spirits.

Both Sandy Desert and the Shumway house lay within the boundaries of Hobbomocko's Hollow, near Trading Cove on the Thames River north of Mohegan Hill. Hobbomocko, "He is bad," is known to New England Indians as a horrible spirit. Fidelia Fielding used to appease such dark beings with gift offerings left at a site near the hollow called White Rock. Still, awful things continued to happen there, and old folks told young Mohegans to avoid the hollow. John Tantaquidgeon once saved a woman from being raped there by an invisible assailant. Gladys recalls her own childhood terror at that place when she ran out of trolley money and ran lightning-quick back up Mohegan Hill.

Family standing was another shadowy topic. John and Harriet Tantaquidgeon were just as responsible for earning their daughter's eventual high rank in the Mohegan tribe as was Gladys herself. Standing in the tribe was not generally something that came about through the actions of any one generation. On her mother's side, the Fieldings spawned many chiefs. Her father's family, the Tantaquidgeons, had earned the ancient right to wear the Hand of Capture symbol. That emblem, of an open hand, honored their ancestor, Tantaquidgeon, "Going along fast." That first Tantaquidgeon was a swift seventeenth-century runner credited with apprehending the Narragansett sachem Miantonomo—a great opponent of Sachem Uncas. Since it "took a chief to take a chief," Tantaquidgeon had to wait for Uncas to arrive before Miantonomo's capture was official.

You had the chiefs' class, and then the warriors and others. Then the third group made up of those who might have been taken as captives and were allowed to live within the group. The third group could not take part in the council or anything of that sort and that did persist.

I know at one point—it didn't mean a great deal to me, I didn't understand it probably—that someone married so-and-so; there might not be very much comment about it. But you got the idea "that wasn't the thing to do."

One good example of how that persisted until probably the 1940s, thereabouts: my father and elderly aunt, who had lived with us for many years and was mother's older sister, Gertrude Harris—we had a large grape arbor out in the back, and it was a nice place for them to sit. So this day father and Aunt Gertrude were sitting under the shade there, and this very fine-looking young man came along . . . he was tracing his roots . . . They didn't reveal that they knew these families that he mentioned. So he didn't gain much from that conversation. So when he left, after a few minutes Aunt Gertrude said,... "I know that name, but we never had much to do with those people." So there was always that kind of thing in the background. It was there.

Maintaining standing required upholding duty and responsibility generation after generation. John and Harriet always took time out from their child rearing, chores, artwork, and storytelling to care for the old folks on the hill. Mohegans view elders as fragile gemstones who preserve the integrity of their ancient lifeways.

When we were young, we always respected and cared for the old folks. All of the elders brought baskets with them when they came visiting. When they left, the baskets were always full. That is how we cared for our old folks.

Young Gladys understood the value of her elders' teachings. At a time in life when most young people have a great deal of freedom, she accepted the path of duty.

As a teen-ager I worked to earn money as a photographer's developing assistant. He took pictures of Mohegans at Fort Shantok, with Chief Occum and Chief Matahga, Cousin Myrtice, Loretta Fielding (daughter of Burrill Fielding). He enlarged photos and sold them. For one large one he had a raffle. Some were sold during the Wigwams.

I also worked at Woolworths and helped take care of the younger children and did dressmaking for a few friends. I did a great deal of sewing for my younger sisters. My younger sister Ruth was born in 1909. At ten till teen-age, I had a great deal of responsibility, because my mother worked away from home at domestic work—at two or three homes.

Gertrude Harris and Loretta Fielding were my best friends. Loretta and Gertrude had more free time and other interests. There were certain boys in the community. But I always had too many other things going on.

CHAPTER 3

ROCK WOMAN

In the Mohegan language, the spirit of rocks is acknowledged in the names for our leaders: a male leader is called *sachem* (which means rock man) and a woman leader is referred to as *sunqsquaw* (which translates as rock woman).

—GLADYS TANTAQUIDGEON

The tales of the elders are as old as the rocks on Mohegan Hill. Those rocks are the bones of Mother Earth. Streaked with quartz crystal veins, they contain hidden messages that guide generation after generation of those who listen well.

Behind Fort Hill, the nanus (respected elder women of the tribe)[6] showed Gladys Cochegun Rock, the largest freestanding boulder in New England. During her youth, six stone seats remained on top. There, they told her, in the seventeenth century, the Mohegan sachem Uncas held council with his men. His most notable decision was to ensure his people's security by allying them with the English newcomers. Early interaction between New England's Indians and Europeans resulted in the extermination of most Connecticut tribes through plague or warfare. Cochegun Rock reminded Gladys of the difficult decisions leaders make to ensure the survival of their people. She also learned that the rock was named for Caleb Cochegan.

[He] used to live there, in a cave under the rock, with a herd of sheep.

Stony Brook runs near Cochegun Rock. On one miraculous day in the eighteenth century, a thundercloud appeared from a clear sky in the shape

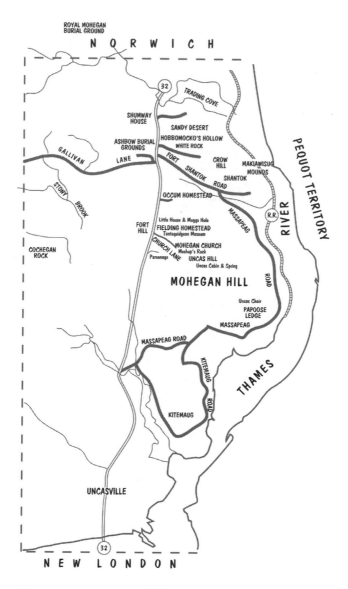

Mohegan territory, circa 1900.

of a hand. That story reflects the Creator's awesome power to effect change. Gladys helped record what her elders said:

Now there came a time when an Indian man was a preacher here. He was Samuel Ashbow. He was a good man, but his wife was not a very good woman, being fond of [unkupi] (rum). For many years she was thus, and it made poor Ashbow very unhappy.

Then there came a certain time when something was going to happen, when something was going to happen from the sky. The Indians were helping a white man build a mill over on Stony Brook, and Ashbow used to go and help too. One time he took his wife along with him. Ashbow was a good man, but his wife had a bottle of [unkupi] hidden in her dress. She began to drink and gave some to the other men. Ashbow watched her only a little while but soon got angry and, taking the rum from her, threw it on a rock. It broke, and the rum spilled on the earth. The wife became furious, and a few moments later, while Ashbow was stooping over a stone, she picked up a piece of rock and struck him on the forehead. He fell down with the blood streaming from him. Then there was a clap of thunder from above, and all looked up, only to see a clear sky with a patch of cloud overhead only as large as a hand. It was a sign to Ashbow's wife, and from that time on she never drank rum; neither did the other men who heard the thunder. Ashbow got well.[7]

The nanus taught Gladys that the Fort Hill rocks, across the street from her home, had the power to protect Mohegans from outsiders. From those guardian rocks, Gladys learned that her ancestors were ever watchful.

Whenever anyone unfriendly passes by who poses a danger to the Mohegan people, Uncas sends rocks down from the hill to fall upon them.

To ensure Uncas's continued protection, young Gladys made offerings at Uncas Spring atop Uncas Hill (across the road from Fort Hill). There, icy cold pure water surfaced from beneath a capped flat-topped rock. The magical powers of that water were renowned. She remembers that her guides told her,

"This water makes one strong and healthy. People travel from afar to get it."

They instructed her to leave a cup there, in case anyone needed a drink. This was the place where Gladys came to understand the importance of giving thanks through maintenance of sacred sites.

Just west of the spring were the stone ruins of Uncas's cabin. Craggy red cedar grew out of those rocks. That fragrant tree stands on the most treasured Mohegan lands. At the cabin, Gladys left gifts, cleaned away brush and leaf debris, and gained reassurance from the lingering spirits of her ancestors.

Devils Rock is a short walk east of Uncas Spring. That three-toed, footprint-shaped impression is mysteriously forever full of water. In spite of its name and the inexplicable water, that stone is in no way evil. Europeans misnamed it. Before they arrived it was known as Moshup's Rock. Moshup is the ancient giant of New England, who lives along the seashores near the whales.

Indian sites were often referred to as such, places of the devil, in order to denigrate them.

Not far from Moshup's Rock, Mohegan Church sits atop Mohegan Hill beside a pile of rock rubble. This was a sacred site long before Mohegans built their Christian church and ages before the English introduced Christianity to the hill. Prior to the building of the church, the tribe held the Wigwam festival on that site at the end of each corn harvest, beneath a giant chestnut tree. After the church was erected in 1831, those Wigwams continued under a brush arbor in front of the sanctuary. Mohegan Church reminded Gladys that sacred places are unaffected by the man-made structures set upon them. What makes them sacred are the rocks and earth beneath.

At this lofty point, Gladys's mentor, Medicine Woman Emma Baker, taught her the story of where her Mohegan people came from. Just as Emma's own mentor had done, she pointed and said,

We came from upstate New York by way of the hills of Taughannock.

Moshup, the giant whose footprint marks Mohegan Hill, has a wife named Granny Squannit, who is the leader of the Makiawisug. She and these Little People of the Woodlands are responsible for earthen mounds on the river's shores east of Mohegan Hill. Gladys's elders were particularly fond of Granny because she aided Mohegan women in the growing of corn, gathering of medicinal herbs, and securing of romantic favors. Learning the ways of the Little People reminded Gladys that elusive beings hold great power and should be remembered through offerings and ceremony. Tribal Faith Keeper Fidelia Fielding told her,

There used to be a lot of Little People around. We call them Makiawisug. You need to leave them small baskets filled with meat, berries, and corn bread. If you leave them in the woods, they will always be gone by the next day.

Just down the lane from the church, abutting Gladys's home, is a Muggs Hole, an ancient stone structure used in more recent times for cold storage of root crops. After the coming of the Europeans, Indian hunting grounds dwindled, making those preservable root crops Mohegan staples. In Gladys's youth, her family served parsnips and sweet potatoes blackened just right in a cast-iron pan. Rutabaga was mashed, seasoned, and baked until sweet. Potatoes were scalloped or mashed with carrots, onions, and cabbage and fried up in a hash. Tribal elders told Gladys,

The stone Muggs Holes are very old. They are found all over. We used to use them for cold storage.

Muggs Holes showed Gladys that her people had built things out of stone that were far older than the renowned colonial buildings in the nearby towns of Norwich, New London, Mystic, and Lebanon.

South of the hill at Massapeag, her teachers taught Gladys about true vigilance. A stone chair nestles into that hillside. As an old man in poor health, Uncas sat there and listened for the paddles of his friends and enemies as they passed along the Thames. Uncas asked his men to carry him to that spot, refusing to abandon his duties. Uncas Chair was where Gladys came to understand that true Mohegans never retire from service to their people.

Nearby is Papoose Rock. At that site, Gladys heard about the dangers of leaving the safety of one's people. Long ago, her elders said,

A Montauk Indian woman had become desolate after leaving her people. In her grief, she took the life of her child by dashing its head against the rocks, leaving them forever a bloody red color.

Farther north along the river is Fort Shantok. Long ago, among the cattails lay a large stone called Shantok Rock. That rock gave way to railroad tracks in the nineteenth century. Gladys's elders showed her that spot where Mohegans had landed following Uncas's seventeenth-century split from the Pequots, reminding her that political discord can forever divide a nation.

Mohegans and Pequots are the same tribe. There is no difference. Uncas was banished from the Pequots and came to live on this side of the river with his followers. Many thought he should have been made sachem of the Pequots.

Upon leaving the Pequots, Sachem Uncas established a fortified village at Shantok, visible in Gladys's youth only as circular and diamond-shaped piles of gritstone and oyster shell. Near the village ruins, her guides showed her hundreds of fieldstones marking the graves of ancestors whose bones had sprouted sacred red cedar trees. Some graves dated from more than four hundred years ago; others were of recently passed tribespeople. Old burials faced southwest toward the origins of the Mohegan people and the sacred corn plant. This Shantok village site also marked the location of eighteenth-century conflicts in which Mohegans withstood assaults from the neighboring Narragansett tribe. Gladys's elders explained that Shantok was a place of great protection, where only good spirits dwelt.

In her youth, the stones at Shantok spoke to Gladys.

One day, I found a perfectly shaped stone axe head protruding from the river's shore at Shantok, at the old village. I remember thinking that it was a sign to protect those things of the past.

North of Shantok, in Norwich, lay the great waterfall of the Yantic River beside the site called Uncas Leap. Uncas jumped that enormous chasm in the 1600s to avoid capture by the Narragansett Indians. Near that precipice, Gladys's ancestor, Tantaquidgeon, caught the Narragansett sachem Miantonomo. At the leap, Gladys learned that ancient spirits can work miracles to protect Mohegan people.

The encounter between the Mohegan and the Narragansett was back in about 1643, thereabouts . . . The Mohegans were outnumbered and . . . being outnumbered, Uncas told his men that he would ask Chief Miantonomo that the two men fight with their clubs man to man. If Miantonomo didn't agree, Uncas said he would fall on his face and his men would charge the enemy— which they did, because Miantonomo said his men came to fight and they

Uncas Leap, Norwich, Connecticut, circa 1940. Chief Matahga (Burrill Fielding), at right, is gesturing to the place where Uncas lept.

would fight. And from that point in the east great plain section of Norwich, they made their way over the falls of the Yantic. The Mohegan runner Tantaquidgeon, whose name means Going along fast on the land or in the water, was the first to lay hands on Miantonomo for Uncas. The site is now referred to as Indian Leap. Some refer to it as Uncas Leap, for Uncas is said to have jumped across.

CHAPTER 4

GIANTS AND LITTLE PEOPLE

There was an Indian and his wife who lived near here long ago....
One stormy night there was a rap on their door. When the woman
opened the door, the wind blew very hard. Someone was standing
outside, but she did not know who it was.... she found out ...
that someone wanted her to take care of a sick woman a long way
off.... The person was a dwarf, but she thought he was a boy. He
led her far away through the storm. After a while they reached a
small underground house.... and there lay a dwarf woman ill on a
bed of skins. The Indian woman then recognized them as [M]akia-
wisug. She stayed with them some time and cared for the sick one
until she got well. When she was ready to return home, the dwarf
gave [her] a lot of presents, blindfolded her, and led her back to
her home. She was very well treated.

—FAITH KEEPER FIDELIA FIELDING, FLYING BIRD[8]

Deep underground, within the rocks of Mohegan Hill, dwell the Makia
wisug, the Little People of the Woodlands. They are hard and bulky and
born of stone. In the mornings, they leave out their laundry as dewy webs
upon the grass. To protect their feet, they pick lady's slipper flowers to wear
as moccasins. Gladys Tantaquidgeon first heard of them from her great-
aunt Fidelia Fielding, who taught that the Little People are among the oldest watchers of the hill. True appreciation of their worth set Gladys apart
from other children and proved her best suited for the medicine trail. She
passed her elders' "first test" on the day she heard about these tiny beings:

The most interesting part of Fidelia's life that I recall was that she knew about the Little People who live in the woods, the Makiawisug. . . . On one occasion there was a family dinner and meeting in the old parsonage, half a mile down the road from here. At one point, she told one of the relatives that she was stepping outside for a minute to talk to the Little People, "someone in the tree."

Some of the younger family members regarded her as "quite different" (and they laughed, but I did not). She used to visit my parents because they didn't ridicule her. Others didn't sympathize with her contact with the Little People.

Because Gladys did not laugh, Fidelia chose to teach her about the Little People and passed on to her an ancient belt that symbolized responsibility to the tiny ones.

It was Fidelia who left me that very old belt that I wear with my Indian dress. It had belonged to her grandmother, Martha Uncas. Martha taught her the Mohegan language. Fidelia Fielding was the last speaker of our Mohegan-Pequot dialect. She and her grandmother . . . lived together. They were said to have used the Indian tongue more than English.

Four semicircular symbols of earth domes, representing the four directions and the concentrated spiritual force of the universe, adorn that belt. On either side of the domes is a beaded trail beside the Tree of Life. Fidelia taught Gladys that this sacred tree grows from the earth to the sky, reaching out from Mother Earth to the celestial beings.

Included with this gift of the well-decorated belt were certain responsibilities. Fidelia made clear to Gladys that protecting the Makiawisug was hard work. She explained that certain rules were absolute:

1. If you see any Makiawisug, avert your gaze; otherwise, they might point at you, become invisible, and ransack your belongings.

2. Leave the Makiawisug offering baskets of berries, cornbread, or meat from time to time.

3. Never speak of them in summer, when they are out and about. Your remarks will insult them.

4. Be good to their leader, Granny Squannit, for she is very old, very powerful, and very wise.[9]

Gladys received Fidelia's teachings until Fidelia's life trail carried her west, when Gladys was only eight years old. Eight decades later, Gladys recalled:

Fidelia Fielding liked to be called by her Indian name, Jeets Bodernasha, which means Flying Bird. She lived about a mile east from our house. It was the last of the log houses on the reservation and she used to refer to it as a tribe house.

Flying Bird (Fidelia Fielding) attending a Wigwam festival, circa 1908.

She was what we would think of as a true full-blood Indian type. She was a little over five feet tall and of medium build. She had jet black hair, black eyes, high cheekbones, and she used to wear a calico dress. In cool weather, she wore capes.

She didn't participate in the Wigwam (green corn festival) and meetings of the women in the Church Ladies Sewing Society. She was very much a loner, very much to herself. Fidelia was not pleased with non-Indian neighbors.

Children in school were expected to learn English and forget all about their Indian cultural background. If some of the older women (like Fidelia) were speaking and some of the children appeared, they would cease talking because they didn't want the children to be punished for learning the Mohegan language.

Linked with lessons on the Little People are tales of Moshup the Giant. Granny Squannit, leader of the Little People, was married to Moshup, and together they raised a family of twelve children:

Whenever there is a terrible storm that means that Moshup and Granny are fighting.

Granny holds dominion over small creatures like spiders, crickets, and clams while also governing the herbs and plant people. By contrast, Moshup is master of the eastern seaboard, where he is king of the whales, greatest of all sea creatures. He can leave footprint impressions upon boulders with a simple step. Moshup is great like the whale. Granny is small like the spider.

Moshup and Granny symbolize one of the great clashes of the medicine world. There is an eternal conflict between large and powerful creatures and little beings of great medicine. Gladys's elders taught that tiny spiders could be as deadly or as beneficial as the mighty whales and that each one had its own valuable medicine. Spiderwebs protect against harmful insects and can be used to heal bleeding wounds. Mohegan women invoke spiders for powerful spiritual protection. Mohegan men are connected to the sea by hunting whales. In some stories about Moshup, members of his family are transformed from humanoids into whales, symbolizing the ancient bonds between land and sea creatures. Gladys learned that sometimes we misunderstand both the very big and the very little. Big beings like Moshup may frequently seem altogether dangerous, rather than mighty, because they can inadvertently destroy small things simply by passing through. So too, we sometimes wrongly attribute to little creatures qualities such as slyness and frailty, rather than the positive traits of agility and delicacy.

Gladys was always small in physical stature, but the lessons of Moshup and Granny's conflicts taught her to reject judgments based on appearances. Her great-aunt Emma Baker explained to her that fear of Moshup's great size had resulted in early Christian missionaries labeling him a devil. When non-Indians first came to Mohegan, they fearfully eradicated all creatures of great size and strength, such as the once abundant bear and moose.

Emma Baker taught Gladys that her ancestors had built Mohegan Church near the site of Moshup's footprint rock because that was a place of special medicine, not an evil one. Emma was a Christian and led the Church Ladies Sewing Society. But as a medicine woman, she also questioned missionary teachings when they denied time-honored Mohegan beliefs. No creatures as evil as the devil of Christianity had ever inhabited the ancient Mohegan world. In her time Gladys worked hard to exorcize the devils that Europeans had brought to Mohegan Hill.

Emma's teachings allowed Gladys to discern, in her youth, that the footprints she found at Devils Hopyard in Moodus, Connecticut, belonged to Moshup. She knew that Devils Hopyard was merely the European name erroneously given to a place where Moshup had walked long ago. He furiously stomped those impressions throughout Connecticut and Massachusetts after a monster crab pinched his toe as he was attempting to build a bridge between Martha's Vineyard and Massachusetts. Moshup's irritation also prompted him to throw stones all over Connecticut, which is why it is so rocky. Little People, giants, huge crabs, and the creation of geological features suggest that the nanu stories reach back over eons. The nanus have a long memory, and they carry with them the knowledge of many lifetimes.

CHAPTER 5

NANU MAGIC

Mohegans and other Algonquian peoples teach certain selected
individuals their pharmacopoeia, magical science, and magical
theory.

—GLADYS TANTAQUIDGEON

In Gladys's youth, some nanus taught and cared for many children on
the hill. Others chose to teach only a few, or even a lone child, a specific
skill. That is the nature of traditional Mohegan education. While Gladys's
great-aunt Fidelia Fielding loathed non-Indians, and nearly all other
Mohegans, on Gladys she lavished her unique gifts and attention. Fidelia
was the last fluent speaker of the Mohegan-Pequot dialect. She was also
the last person to live in an old-style tribe house, a log dwelling. Fidelia
involved herself only with those who could preserve the old ways. Prefer-
ring the Mohegan name Jeets Bodernasha (which means Flying Bird), she
respected the traditional upbringing Gladys had received from her parents.

Fidelia taught Gladys the more difficult side of Mohegan magic and
medicine. Those weighty teachings balanced the lighter medicine offered
to her by the other bright-spirited women she called her three grandmothers: her great-aunt Medicine Woman Emma Baker, her maternal
grandmother, Lydia Fielding, and a Nehantic woman named Mercy Ann
Nonesuch Mathews. These three women began Gladys's formal training
in 1904, when they first took her into the medicine fields. She has never
forgotten the glorious day when they chose her to become the next
Mohegan medicine woman.

My first trip out to the fields—where medicine plants were growing—that would have been with Grandma Fielding, Grandmother Baker, and Grandmother Mathews. They were gathering plants for winter use, and at that time, I would have been about five years of age. I think it kindled a spark. Later on, I became interested in our Mohegan herbal remedies.

Here, in my recollection, the women were the ones who gathered the plants and prepared the medicines. It was customary in herb gathering and other things that the women would observe some of the girls. They would discuss them, saying, "Perhaps it might be well to take this one to learn certain skills." Then they would select someone.

In connection with the Wigwam (brush arbor festival), my great-aunt Emma Baker selected her niece, Nettie Fowler, and I assisted her (and I was *her* niece). Then I was selected. And so in later time, I worked as her vice-president in the Church Ladies Sewing Society which organized the Wigwam festival. Then it went from aunt to niece, and that might hold true now, and I might skip a generation.

Of all Gladys's nanus, Emma Baker held the highest standing within the Mohegan Tribe. She was married to a Mohegan man named Henry, and together they had six children. Emma became medicine woman after the death of her grandmother and mentor, Martha Uncas, in 1859. She held that position until her own passing in 1916. Emma also chaired the tribal council from 1897 to 1902 and was president of the Mohegan Church Ladies Sewing Society throughout the late nineteenth and early twentieth centuries.

Long before American women could vote, Emma boldly represented her people in front of an all-white male Connecticut legislature. The lawmakers acknowledged her as "a very intelligent woman of the tribe." Nanu Baker kept meticulous records of disputed lands and maintained extensive tribal genealogies. She preserved much of Mohegan tribal history in written and spoken form during a time when it was doubtful that any future Mohegans would care. By passing on to Gladys her tribe's history, in both written form and the oral tradition, Emma chronicled where the Mohegans had come from and prescribed where they had to go.

Mercy Mathews and Lydia Fielding joined Emma in cultivating Gladys's understanding of tribal portents and healing practices. Their lessons were fleeting, however, for they all passed away before she reached adulthood. Yet Gladys spent the rest of her life traveling east to west and back again to complete the path that her three grandmothers set for her. Following the healing trail required her to observe the basic woodland code the nanus had taught her. She remembered, for example, that a healer should dispense water in a turtle shell cup when administering herbal treatment.

Sometimes they gathered as many as ten different plants to effect a single cure. They taught me never to gather during the hot dog days of August and never to pick more than you need. They always practiced conservation.

In the spring, early plants were referred to as weeds, and they were gathered and cooked as greens—a spring tonic: dandelion, poke, milkweed, plantain, and dock, to name a few. Other plants were more important as sources of healing ingredients, such as bloodroot, boneset, motherwort, ginseng. Plants were gathered and carefully dried in the sun. The sun adds to their potency. Some plants are actually poison when green. They are dried, ground with a stone or wooden mortar, and gathered.

The most critical nanu lesson was the prohibition against bad medicine. Nanus allowed only good medicine for healing or other magical purposes. No ceremony could hold ill intent for anyone. Her three grandmothers taught Gladys that if she failed to use only good medicine under all circumstances the spirits could make her medicine forever tainted and ineffective, causing herself and her people grave harm.

To ensure continued good medicine practices, they taught her to surround herself with things that brought good spirits—such as cedar, quartz, sweet grass, tobacco, corn, silver, and ancient artifacts. Fidelia also reminded her to make periodic offerings to the Makiawisug. Such protections and practices were the tools of her trade. They were weapons with which to battle the *muci mundo,* or bad spirits, who caused illness, accidents, tribal discord, and personal troubles.

Gladys's three grandmothers also taught her to bead wall pockets (hanging storage compartments for sewing supplies), floral regalia collars, and velvet pincushions with the protective symbols of good medicine. They

Gladys, wearing regalia borrowed from another tribe, poses with herbs for Frank Speck, circa 1911.

passed down the meaning of the ageless designs of diamonds, trails, earth domes, and four directional markings. Certain designs were forbidden—such as vivid depictions of animals—as was using too much of the color green. Similarly, certain feathers, such as those of the eagle, were reserved for ceremonies and high honors. Owl feathers were forbidden except in rare instances, for the owl's cry is an omen of death. Tradition did not permit using such heavy medicine for simple decoration.

Through their teaching of these protective practices and arts, Gladys learned the meanings of the symbols in Mohegan handiwork and ceremonies. For example, a Trail of Life symbol, with an arrow pointing east to west, explained the east-to-west passage of spirits, akin to the movement of the sun. As Gladys beaded that design, the east-west openings in the ceremonial arbor for the Wigwam festival suddenly made sense. When her three grandmothers made her first regalia, they beaded it with floral and leaf patterns, signifying the healing woodland plants that would be her pharmacopoeia. The central symbol found on her regalia is

the familiar four[-]domed medallion, or so-called rosette.... Four domes could represent the four directions that guide the traveler or call the winds. Central to these, the space that is of the spirit could be represented as a dot, circle[,] or a combination of these elements. To this basic symbol, artists might add representations of their own primary considerations—family, tribal members, plants for food and medicine[,] or the trails and paths traveled.[10]

CHAPTER 6

REPRESENTING THE ANCESTORS

We, the Mohegan Tribe of Indians of Connecticut, answerable to our ancestors, in order to secure to ourselves and our descendants the management of our own affairs as a sovereign American Indian Nation, to ensure the maintenance of our basic human rights, to exercise our sovereign rights as a federally recognized Indian tribe including the right of self-determination and self-governance, and to promote the general welfare of the Mohegan people, do hereby establish, adopt, and proclaim this Constitution.

—Preamble to the Mohegan Constitution, 1996

A modern-day sign outside Gladys's childhood home reads "Mohegan, Seat of Uncas, the Mohegan Sachem, Friend of the English." Out of necessity, Mohegans opted for friendship with the powerful English newcomers in the seventeenth century.

The members of those English families through the years have continued to be friendly with the Mohegans. For example, way back, General William Williams (one of the prominent families of Norwich) visited with the Mohegans and would attend church service. So did Ernest Rogers and the Rogers family, the Hyde family, and any number of families. My grandparents and some of the elders would come and tell us about these friendships.

That ancestral commitment has required constant maintenance. Representing the tribe at non-Indian events like town anniversaries, pageants, and parades is an ongoing testing ground for Mohegan leaders. Gladys

Tantaquidgeon eventually represented her people so well, both at home and across the country, that she became the archetypal Mohegan ambassador.

Her ability to attract good spirits offered her critical protection when representing her people at places of terrible evil. One such site is the Royal Mohegan Burial Ground of Norwich, Connecticut. As a child, Gladys was chosen to stand for her people there, just as her predecessor, Medicine Woman Emma Baker, had done. Emma was only a young woman when she witnessed a horrific desecration of Mohegan bones and bodies at that place. Similar disturbances eventually reduced that sixteen-acre burial area to a scant one-eighth of an acre. She remembered going with her mother to the corner of Sachem and Washington streets

in the fall of 1842. Where Mr. Osgood[']s house now stands[,] someone had plowed and set out cabbages. Mother said it was the first time that she ever saw it plowed and she would like to know who did it. We then went across the ravine[,] and on the edge of it someone had made a pit and had a piece of pipe in it for the smoke to escape[,] and they were burning some of the bones and bodies which they had dug up when they had commenced building the Goddard Cottage. We then walked across the ravine, and there was a large plain lot then which had not been built on. She said the burying ground went beyond that and that they had commenced to build on some of the land. She said that when [she was] 14 years old she worked in the city and used to come there to look at the graves. From Yantic Street clear round to the monument[,] they were as thick as they could be. When the cellar was dug for the house Mr. Newton Perkins built, they found many remains of Indians[,] which verified her word about the graves. . . . I heard Mr. Fitch[,] my grandmother[,] and mother talking about the graveyard[,] and they asked him to go and stop their building. Oh, he said, I did not know you cared about it[,] and he said he would see about it. He was the [Indian] Agent or Overseer and that was all he did do . . . talk about it. (December 14, 1897)[11]

When Emma told Gladys that grisly story, Gladys knew she would one day uphold the dignity of her ancestors at that place. She also recognized that the molestaton and removal of their remains and the theft of their headstones could not erase their memory. On the 250th anniversary of Uncas's grant of Norwich to the English, Gladys first accepted her responsibility to that site. Although only ten years old, she reached out to those who had journeyed west along the Path of the Sun toward the Beautiful White Path, those whose dead bodies had been brutalized.

The childhood event that I recall most vividly was in 1909. There was a celebration in Norwich. On many different occasions, Mohegan Indians would be honored in Norwich and New London and served dinners and would meet various dignitaries.... In those days, we had horse-drawn hacks, and there were five of us. There was a long parade and quite a number of men on foot. President Taft was there, and we were introduced. I shook hands with him. I was impressed with the governor's Foot Guard. I was ten and with one of my cousins. She was with her grandmother, and I was with my grandmother.

The burying grounds at Shantok, along the tranquil Thames, starkly contrast with the dark turmoil of that Norwich burial ground beside the rushing Yantic River. At Shantok, Mohegans have long laid their kin to rest. There Gladys learned the ancient rituals of caring properly for the dead. She watched Fleetfoot (Lloyd Gray) guide the ceremonial pipe through the four directions, while her uncle, Chief Matahga (Burrill Fielding), placed arrowheads beside fallen warriors. She witnessed elders offer tobacco and food to the spirits of the deceased. Some left behind stones for remembering. Most important, she heard Lester Skeesucks call the ancestors to convey the deceased westward along their ultimate trail:

Yu ni ne ne un dai;
ji-bai o-ke ni ki pi ai;
ni mus se chu.

Gladys representing her tribe at a local non-Indian gathering, circa 1913.

> (Here I am;
> To the spirit land I am coming;
> I shall pass away.)

Darkness and light flicker through all passages to and from the Trail of Life,
the Path of the Sun, and the Beautiful White Path. But Shantok has always
been more a place of the light than a place of the dark. Those well-blessed
and peaceful grounds provided Gladys with enough light to carry with her
everywhere.

CHAPTER 7

POUNDING YOKEAG

The men and women who were steeped in the tradition ... who were passing on the tradition ... [were the ones] who knew the tradition of yokeag.

—JAYNE FAWCETT, vice-chair, Mohegan Tribal Council

Mohegans know that corn feeds the spirit and the body. It is placed with the dead to give them spiritual sustenance. In olden times, Mohegan women fostered the growth of corn plants with prayer, offerings, and proper preparation.

There were also many rules for planting. ... The three sisters—corn, beans, and squash—need extra care. ... It must be planted when the dogwood leaves are the size of a squirrel's ear. The seeds are soaked in water overnight before planting. White beans must be planted when the chestnut trees are in full bloom, and squash should be planted when the moon is waxing.[12]

Elders enhanced the spiritual potency of corn when they transformed it into sweet, crunchy *yokeag*, through sun drying, followed by grinding with a mortar and pestle. The substance was far more than simple cornmeal. Mohegans, in ancient times, guarded yokeag in containers with sacred designs, such as diamond medicine symbols. Long ago, when Mohegan men left on long hunting trips, they carried yokeag in leather pouches as their journey cake or traveling food. Pounding that yokeag was an activity performed by each generation of Mohegans. It connected them with those who had gone before. Gladys's tribal standing, as affirmed by her nanus, earned her the right to pound yokeag at a young age. Through understanding the power of the mortars, pestles, and corn needed to create it, she realized her true place in the universe.

In Mohegan stories, corn, mortars, and pestles are recurring motifs. One of the most important stories taught to Gladys by Fidelia Fielding was the "Tale of Chahnameed." This story dates back more than four hundred years and features the role of mortars and pestles in the lives of Mohegan women. References to these tools suggest corn (*wiwacumunx*) in its ground form as yokeag. The anthropologist Frank Speck recorded Fidelia's version in 1902:[13]

The Tale of Chahnameed

Long ago there lived a man upon an island some distance from the mainland. His name was Chahnameed, he was a great eater, a glutton. On the island he had a house, and in a cove near by he kept two canoes. One day, as he stood on the beach looking toward the mainland, he saw something moving, but he could not make out what it was. He looked for some time, and then saw that it was a beautiful young girl walking along the beach. He said to himself: "She is looking for shells to put upon her dress"; for her garment was of buckskin covered with colored beads, shells, and fringe. She was very beautiful, and Chahnameed thought so. So he put his hands about his mouth, and called to her. When she looked up, he called to her, and asked her to come over and live with him. The girl hesitated, but Chahnameed urged her, and at last she consented. Then he got out one of his canoes, and paddled to the mainland. When he got there, the girl said: "I will come back but first I must go and get my mortar and pestle." So she went away to her village, and Chahnameed waited for her. When she came back, she had a mortar, a pestle[,] and some eggs. Then he took her in the canoe, and paddled to the island, and after that they lived together for a long time.

Now Chahnameed was accustomed to stay away from home for long periods, during which his wife did not know what he did, or where he went. She did not like this, but said nothing to him about it. After a while, however, she made up her mind that she would leave him, for she did not like to be left alone so long. Quietly she set about making some dolls. She made a great many, decorating them with paint and shells, but one doll was made larger than the rest. These she put away, so that her husband should not find them. Waiting until he had departed as usual one day, she took her mortar and pestle and some eggs down to the canoe. This canoe Chahnameed had left at home. Then she went back to the house, and got the dolls, which she put against the walls in different places, all facing the center. The large one she put on the bed, and covered it up with robes. Before she left, she put a little dried dung about each doll, and then crawled into bed, and voided her excrement where the doll lay. She then left her handiwork, went down to the canoe, and paddled towards the mainland. In the canoe were the mortar, the pestle[,] and eggs.

By and by Chahnameed came home. When he got to the house he looked for his wife, but did not find her. Then he went in and looked around. He saw the dolls, and went over towards one. Immediately the one against the wall began to scream. When he turned around to look at it, the first one began to scream. Every time he turned to look at one doll, the one that was behind him would begin to scream. He did not know what they were. Soon he saw that something was in the bed, and, taking a big stick, he went over to it. He struck the large doll that was under the robes, thinking that it might be his wife. The large doll then screamed louder than the others. He pulled down the robes, and saw that it was only a doll. Then he threw down his stick, and ran down to his canoe. He knew that his wife had departed, for he saw that the mortar and pestle were gone.

When he got to the shore, he put his hands to his eyes, and looked for a long time toward the mainland. Soon he saw her paddling very hard for the land. He leaped into his canoe, and went after her. He soon began to gain, and before long he was almost up to her, and would have caught her, had she suddenly not crept to the stern of her canoe and lifting up her mortar, thrown it out into the water. Immediately the water where the mortar fell became mortars. When Chahnameed got there, he could go no farther. But he jumped out of his canoe and dragged it over the mortars, then pushed it into the water and jumped into it again. He paddled very hard to catch her up. His wife paddled very hard, too. But again he began to gain, and soon almost caught her. As before, however, she crept back to the stern, and raising the pestle, threw it over. Where it fell, the water became pestles. Then she paddled on again very hard. Chahnameed could not pass these pestles either, so he jumped out and dragged the canoe over them; then jumped in and paddled as hard as he could to catch up. Again he began to gain and almost caught her. But his wife crept to the stern of her canoe, and threw out all the eggs. Where the eggs fell, the water turned to eggs. Chahnameed could not get through these either. So he jumped out and dragged the canoe over them as before. This time he had to work very hard to get through the eggs, but at last succeeded. He paddled harder than ever, and soon began to catch up again. Now he would have caught her, for she had nothing more to throw out. But she stopped paddling and stood up. Quickly she raised her hand to her head, and from the top pulled out a long hair. Then she drew it through her fingers, and immediately it became like a spear. Chahnameed thought he was going to catch her now; he did not see what she was doing. When he got quite near, she balanced the hair-spear in her hand, and hurled it at him. She threw it straight; it hit him in the forehead, and he fell out of the canoe, and sank. He was dead. This all happened a very long time ago, back in the beginning of the world. The woman went back to her people. She was a Mohegan.[14]

In this tale, mortars and pestles invoke individual magic and solidify tribal identity. The Mohegan woman is unnamed because she is only one of many women who have held these powers. When female Mohegans die, mortars and pestles often go with them inside their graves. Cup-shaped carvings at the base of Mohegan mortars reflect the medicine of Grandfather Turtle (on whose back the Great Spirit created the world) and the life-giving powers of Mohegan womanhood. Many mortars and pestles pass from one generation to the next in a sacred chain of remembrance.

At the annual Wigwam, Gladys witnessed her childhood chiefs, Weegun, Fielding, Occum, Peegee Uncas, and Matahga, joining the chain. Each participated in the yokeag ritual along with Emma Baker. The pounding of the yokeag bound men and women into a circle of memory. They taught Gladys that this circle linked her, too. So important was the ritual that even a non-Indian associated it with Chief Matahga, Gladys's uncle Burrill, when he died:

> I thought, "The passing of a Warrior—Burrill H. Fielding—('Bokie!')" "Bokie" supervised the building of the Wigwam—I could smell the drying leaves. "Bokie" helped to pound yokeag with the old mortar and pestle in the backyard. He rang the church bell rousing the gang to get

Gladys beside her family's seventeenth-century mortar and pestle in 1930. The Tantaquidgeon home is at rear.

up and get to work. If this didn't get quick enough results[,] I could hear him coming down the upstairs hall in Nana Quidgeon's [Nanu Tantaquidgeon's] house knocking on all the doors, "Come on! Come on! Time to get to work!" He made the succotash and clam chowder at the Wigwam, standing over a black kitchen stove on a hot August day.[15]

The Wigwam (green corn festival) was the annual focus of tribal activity in Gladys's youth. At that celebration, those who held a special place in the tribal community pounded yokeag. They connected each generation of Mohegans with ancestors who had done that same act for that same reason for thousands of years.

CHAPTER 8

WELCOME TO THE WIGWAM

The nanus taught that the very word *Wigwam* is inviting; it comes from the Mohegan expression *Wigwomun,* which means Come into my home.

The Mohegan year cycles from Wigwam to Wigwam. Yet for some years, the Wigwam had not been held. Non-Indian ways had spread among the people. The corn harvest was no longer central to their lives. Tribespeople were becoming negligent in their maintenance of Mother Earth and her rock sites. Old stories of Granny Squannit were treated as archaic superstitions by most Mohegans. Many ceased to leave offerings at Uncas Spring and Moshup's Rock. But during Gladys's youth, Mohegans had a Wigwam because Emma Baker's late mother, Rachel, had told Emma to save that festival.

Rachel knew that the planned dissolution of the Mohegan Reservation in the mid-nineteenth century would leave the church as the only tribally owned sacred site. Therefore, pre-Christian native ceremonies could only survive in coexistence with the church. Later, Emma had a dream, a dream message from Rachel about the Wigwam. The success of the restoration of that festival convinced Gladys that dream messages from ancestors yield magic strong enough to revive the lifeblood of a people. In the Algonquian Indian language (of which Mohegan speech is a part) the word *pauwau* refers to one who dreams as well as to a medicine person, for the two are synonymous.[16] The power to dream dreams and make them come true is central to Indian medicine. Interestingly, the term *powwow* or *pow wow* (a corruption of that old Indian word for dreams and dreamers) is used for Indian festivals across the country.

The festival of corn requires a full four seasons of preparation. Yokeag is dried, while Mohegans sew piles of ribbons, feathers, fringe, and beads into regalia. To complete her Wigwam preparations, Gladys's nanus painted red circles onto her face in recognition of the corn plant's life energies.

Emma Baker influenced my life at that time in connection with "the ceremonial." She was one of my grandfather Eliphalet Fielding's sisters. Therefore, she was technically my aunt. But she was one of the women whom I used to refer to as grandmother. Lydia Fielding, my maternal grandmother, and Mercy Ann Nonesuch Mathews—she was Nehantic and had married a Mohegan man—they were also my grandmothers. I used to refer to Grandma Baker, Grandma Fielding, and Grandmother Mathews as my three grandmothers. I spent a great deal of time with those three women when I was very young.

Wigwam time was when Gladys learned to be Muhukiniuk, or "One with the spirit of all Mohegans." The event served as a homecoming for non-Indian friends and neighbors as well. The Mohegan expression "Wig-womun" (Come into my home) was implicit in all festival activities.

Even the brush arbor that was the centerpiece of the festival was built with east and west doors to allow spirits following the Path of the Sun to journey comfortably. Beneath the arbor, "fancy tables" featured the work of tribal artists specializing in beading, basketry, and wood carving. Chief Matahga ruled over the cookshack, preparing clear broth clam chowder and succotash made of pink-speckled shell beans, salt pork fat, and yellow corn.

The building of the brush arbor Wigwam structure required . . . hours of hard labor. Eight or ten men cut the poles. This brush arbor was fifty or sixty feet square. It was built in our churchyard. The poles were set eight or ten feet apart, and they were crotched. Grey birch saplings were set across the top and woven across the sides so that it was completely enclosed. There was an entrance section left toward the east, and there was an entrance toward the west, close to the cookhouse. East and west doors had to do with early traditions. The openings provided places for spirits to pass through.

At the east end there would be one of our Mohegan men in his Indian clothes. He would be there to greet people. In early times, it was Chief Occum, Lemuel Fielding. Indoors, there was the person who would take the entrance fee, which was fifteen cents.

There were different tables arranged. First, was the table with penny candy. One of the candies many of us liked was a round coconut candy. The next table was all baked goods, all sorts of cakes and pies.

In the middle of the Wigwam was what they called the fancy table. It had the items that the women made during the year. You could buy a nice gingham apron. There were quite a few baskets made by our Indian men and wooden cooking utensils such as spoons and ladles. One of our women did some beaded purses in floral designs.

The more important tables were where they served the good food. One table served ice cream, and some liked it with yokeag on top.

In the corner was the fortune-teller, she read your palm. Her name was Jeanette Fielding. But if she did not like people, she would not read their palms. She had practiced palmistry for a great many years. She would read your palm for fifteen or twenty cents. Everyone said that she was very good.

Out in the cookhouse, Aunt Nettie and Chief Matahga, with other Mohegans and some of our neighbors, would get the corn husked, peel potatoes, and shell beans. This was an all-day affair—for them, through day and evening.

Some of our elders were basket makers, wood-carvers, and one or two were doing a little beadwork. They didn't think of that in terms of "Mohegan Indian cultural survival." That was just part of everyday life.

Mohegan Church, with a brush arbor frame in front, in 1909.

Welcome to the Wigwam, you will see it in the papers bye and bye,
You miss the chance of your life, if you let it pass you by.
It's the first week in September, 'tis then they have the fair,
They always call it Wigwam, most everybody will be there.

They will meet you, and will greet you, and take you by the hand,
The dinners that you get there are the best that's in the land.
When you enter at the Wigwam 'tis there beside the door,
'Tis then you pay just fifteen cents, they never ask no more.

Moses Fielding used to be there,
And always took the fare,

But he has passed away from Earth,
Another has his chair.

Mrs. Eliphalet Fielding, she will be there, she has a pleasant smile,
She has candles on her table of every kind and style,
She has candles and has peanuts, she will sell at different price,
She will put some in a bag for you and do them up so nice.

Now over in the corner a Palmist there you will find,
She will tell you of the friends you have met and those you have left
    behind.
She will tell you what you are doing and what you ought to do,
She will tell you of friends that have passed away and those that are un-
    true.

Now over on the table there you see the cake so nice,
You can buy it by the loaf, or can buy it by the slice;
Mrs. Harris and Mrs. Skeesucks are waiting there with care
And if you have to stand a minute, they will offer you a chair.
For they have boxes, and have baskets, and paper white as snow;
They will do some up for you and you can take it when you go.

Now over to the fancy table Mrs. Dolbeare and Mrs. Avery you will find,
Also Mrs. Cynthia Fowler, she is so good and kind;
There you see a line of aprons, some white, some striped and light,
And lots of pretty things, I am sure is there in sight;
Also a pile of holders and other fancy work, if you but ask the price.

Now you will go and get your dinner I am sure before you are through,
You will have a plate of chowder, also an oyster stew,
You will want to taste the yokeag and have a plate of cream,
You'll go to the bag and give a grab, I know you will give a scream,
For if you should grab a baby's rattle, a pencil or a pad
If you came there feeling lonely, I am sure it will make you glad.

Mrs. Henry Mathews holds the grab-bag, to her it is not new,
She always is contented when there is something she can do;

When she has passed away from earth we will see a vacant place,
We will miss her tender greeting and her bright and smiling face.

Henry Mathews has passed away, they all do miss him there,
He was deacon of the church for years and often offered prayer
And when they had the Wigwam fair some baskets he would make,
They were so nice and handy they were brought to carry cake.

Donald Meech helps to build the Wigwam and he is always there,
He is so kind and willing he always does his share; he will stand there by
    his table and will serve you with the cream
And sell you too some yokeage, I am sure it is no dream.

John Tantaquidgeon will make some clothes sticks, some scoops and
    wooden spoons.
They will not last long when at the Fair for they are sold too soon.
For the people who go there to buy they think they are so nice,
They always want to take some home, they will pay most any price.

Now Mrs. Isabelle Lemoine and Mrs. Alma Dunn,
For they begin cake-baking before the Fair's begun,
They bake a lot of cookies and bake a lot of pies
And the work I am sure those two can do would be a great surprise.

Eliphalet Fielding used to do the cooking and always did his best
But he has passed away from earth and now he is at rest;
His daughter, Mrs. Fowler, she takes her father's place,
She is so kind and pleasant with a smile upon her face.

Now out there in the cookhouse, 'tis her you there can see,
Her pies and cakes are of the best, with me you will agree;
Also Burrill Fielding, he makes the oyster stew,
If you stop and watch a minute you will see he has a lot of work to do.

Charlie Mathews will husk the corn, Shelly Hunter will shell the beans,
Mrs. Fowler will make the succotash, Oh my! How good it seems.
Mrs. B. H. Fielding stands there waiting to see what she can do,
She will serve you a plate of succotash, or if you wish an oyster stew.

Edwin Fowler is the sexton and you will always find him there,
He lights the lights and makes the fire and keeps the church with care,
But if he should be called away there is none to fill his place,
You will always find him just the same with a smile upon his face.

Now Mrs. Delana Miller was the first President they had,
When you hear them speak of her it is with voice that's sad,
She is absent from among [us;] her work and cares are o'er
But they will meet her bye and bye upon the other shore.

Mrs. Henry Baker now President, and if you wish to see her there
She is over by the window sitting in a chair,
Also her daughter, Emma, she stands right over there,
She waits upon the table and is always at the fair.

Now Lemuel Fielding sings in the Church glad songs of joy,
Telling how our savior when on Earth was once a little boy;
Then people stop and listen, they love to hear him sing.
About our Lord and Savior who on Earth was once a king.[17]

~~~~~~~

PART II

EASTERN TRAIL

CHAPTER 9

THE ANTHROPOLOGIST

As if the Little Ones
had pointed at him,
with his head turned away,
he speaks.

A Messenger comes
a long way carrying
words which he does
not fully understand.

—"THE ANTHROPOLOGIST," from *Mundu*
Wigo: Poems from Mohegan Stories and the Mohegan
Diary of Flying Bird, by Joseph Bruchac

In 1902, a young Columbia University anthropology student named Frank
Goldsmith Speck visited the Mohegans to do ethnographic research. Like
the nanus of Mohegan Hill, Speck saw glimmers of special qualities in a
toddler named Gladys Tantaquidgeon.

When Frank Speck first visited Mohegan, I recall the elders saying that they
liked him very much. I think that was because his theories were in their form-
ative stages. It was our brother Burrill Tantaquidgeon, who was living with
Frank at the old parsonage, who convinced him to meet his aunt Fidelia
Fielding and record the language from her. I do not know how he did it.
Fidelia didn't like many people. . . . When Frank Speck first met me, he said

"Hurry up and grow up little girl, and when I get married I'll come back with my wife and take you away with me." And that was true.

In the decades that followed, Speck transcribed many traditional Mohegan stories never before written down. He made a valued contribution to saving the Mohegan language. Speck recorded it from Fidelia Fielding, who had taught little of it to Gladys because she feared that Gladys would be punished as children had been in her day for speaking their native tongue.

Over the years Fidelia and Gladys's three grandmothers noted her continuing interest in Speck's work and made ready for her inevitable journey away from the hill. Lydia Fielding, Emma Baker, and Mercy Mathews's training included taking Gladys on imaginary trips to faraway places where they posed as strangers who questioned her about her identity. Their goal was to prepare her to represent her people confidently anywhere and under all circumstances. Their trial journeys upstaged any of her "real" travels. In 1911 Speck brought Gladys with his family to New York City, just as he had promised years earlier.

Well, the first trip the Specks took me on was to New York City. When they took me to New York City, they didn't imagine that my Grandmother Lydia Fielding and I had already been on trips to New York in our imaginations. So I wasn't too impressed. We had also made ball dresses to wear to social events in Washington, D.C., for quite some time.

By that time, Gladys's three grandmothers felt it best for her to expand her medicine trail with Speck, who offered her new horizons. She went with his family to live among non-Indian people and soon learned what it meant to be stereotyped as "the Indian girl."

Dr. Speck and his wife, Florence, took me with them on summer vacations—from about 1912 to 1918. The first . . . was when I was twelve years of age. Every

Gladys's three grandmothers—Medicine Woman Emma Fielding Baker, Mercy
Ann Nonesuch Mathews (Nehantic), and Lydia Fielding—working at a Wigwam
festival, circa 1908.

summer after that, for a number of years, and on several occasions, members of our family visited them. Sisters Winifred and Ruth drove to visit them at Hampton Beach, New Hampshire. Our brother Harold spent many weeks with the Speck family.

The Speck home on Cape Ann was a large summer cottage—just a big living room–dining room combination and about four bedrooms downstairs. The basement was where my brother Harold spent time working. He would have his craftwork going on down there.

The first year I visited there, I recall that some of the children, in the families of neighbors in their summer homes, had been told that "an Indian girl from Mohegan, Connecticut, was coming to visit the Specks." And they thought an Indian girl ... would be a great swimmer. I don't know if any word had been spread that my name, Tantaquidgeon, meant going along fast either on land or in the water. We supposed it meant going along fast on land because our ancestor was Tantaquidgeon, the aide to Uncas and a fast runner. They were much disappointed when the first time I was at the beach, "the Indian girl from Mohegan" could not swim a stroke.

Summers with the Specks molded Gladys into an Indian nationalist. She had not previously known many Indians outside Mohegan. At the anthropologist's home at Cape Ann, the chiefs and medicine women who visited were no longer just aunts, uncles, and grandmothers. They were tribal leaders and spokesmen for their respective sovereign nations. They were Gabe Paul, the Penobscot, or Joe Little Bear, the Micmac. She recalls suddenly representing her own tribe fully as "Gladys Tantaquidgeon, the Mohegan." Like all Indians, those tribal "cousins" scrutinized the finer points of intertribal differences to determine one another's relative worth. From that dynamic, Gladys learned that all Indians humorously banter over standing.

With the Specks we visited Penobscot Indian people who came to Magnolia, Massachusetts, to sell baskets—the Paul family at work. And we took visits to Abenaki and Intervale, New Hampshire.

Joe Little Bear, the Micmac, traveled a great deal through the country. If he appeared in New York State, where the group he was performing with was a particular tribe, he'd "change his tribe" to that one: in New York he'd be a Mohawk; out West, a Blackfeet, and so on.

Those learning vacations were my introduction to some of the representatives of other tribes. I always have, and still, think of myself as Mohegan.

CHAPTER 10

EDUCATING ACADEMIA

The Indian didn't talk too good, and the white man didn't hear too good.

—CHIEF HAROLD TANTAQUIDGEON

Frank Speck forever misunderstood the true magic of Mohegan Hill. Always the academic, he once challenged the Old Mohegan Stonecutter. Gladys heard this story from her aunt Nettie Fowler years later:

> One night Dr. Speck was recording some information from Mr. and Mrs. Cooper on Fort Hill. When he had finished, he bid them goodnight. As he said goodbye, they gave one another a puzzled look. Then Mrs. Cooper said to Frank, "[Y]ou can't go home tonight[;] it's a full moon[,] and the [O]ld [S]tonecutter will be out." Frank laughed and said, "Oh[,] don't worry, I'll be fine." Then Mrs. Cooper looked at Mr. Cooper and shrugged as Frank went out the door. After he had gone a little way, he heard a sound as if something was following him. It sounded like the "chink, chink" of an axe. "Well,["] thought Dr. Speck, ["]my imagination has taken hold of me now." So he decided to ignore the noise and keep on going. After he went a little farther, the noise grew much louder and seemed to be getting closer to him. Finally, Dr. Speck had had enough[,] and he ran back to the Cooper[s'] house. When he walked in the door he saw a note beside a candle. It read, "We knew you'd be back, your bed is ready for you. Good night."[18]

Speck soon forgot the Old Stonecutter. Even after experiencing Mohegan magic firsthand, he continued to regard the nanus' spirit teachings as superstitions.

By 1919, Gladys's three grandmothers had all passed away, and at the age of twenty, she chose to investigate the source of his disbelief. Flinging herself into the science of anthropology and academic view of the world, without any formal high school training, she accepted a position as Speck's anthropology assistant at the University of Pennsylvania. There, her life trail became immediately rockier. School had never been the place where she gained wisdom. However, the anthropology curriculum allowed her a great deal of time away from the classroom. Speck frequently sent her to visit eastern tribes as part of her fieldwork. Again, as they had in her childhood, tribal elders led Gladys farther along her trail.

In interpreting indigenous religious practices, Gladys showed acuity; her insights leapfrogged those of Speck. He referred to Fidelia Fielding's comments about the Makiawisug (Little People) and other spiritual subjects as "betray[ing] her biased attitude, religious fanaticism, her moral inconsistency, egoism, and fundamental native superstition."[19] Instead of denigrating Fidelia's beliefs, Gladys instead decided to investigate them fully. She devoted her energies to serious comparisons of Mohegan knowledge with the cosmology of related tribes, such as the Wampanoag.

Her study of the Wampanoag entitled "Notes on the Gay Head Indians of Massachusetts" reflected her understanding. Like Speck, Gladys commented on beliefs in the Little People and their leader Granny Squannit (whom the Wampanoags called Granny Squant) recording that the Gay Head people believed her to be "still alive and frequent[ing] the beaches along the south shore." Further, "It appears that originally she was a supernatural being to whom they prayed for spiritual and material aid." Gladys concluded by saying that the Wampanoags were "inhabiting the sacred territory of their ancestors and living as nearly as possible in accord with their teachings."[20]

The inability of Speck, a longtime student of Mohegan, to comprehend an Indian worldview did not prepare Gladys for the limitations of students at the University of Pennsylvania. The novelty of a grandmother-trained American Indian woman studying anthropology at an Ivy League school prompted misunderstandings and discrimination. The years 1919–26 were not easy.

Gladys's Penobscot friend, Molly Dellis Nelson, also enrolled at the university, affording them both some companionship. Together they cut their long braids into flapper bobs and wore their traditional Indian belts slung low on their hips in 1920s fashion. In spite of those attempts at mainstream style, Gladys and Molly remained conspicuous curiosities. Outside the anthropology department, their social associations were limited to the International House. The university administration had segregated these two brown-skinned indigenous women with the foreign students. They were treated as aliens in their native land:

It was quite an event for students and different faculty members to have two Indian women and particularly from New England, because so much more is known about Indians from other parts of the country. Molly lived on campus, and I lived with the Specks. Molly, after two or three years, continued to study dance and went on to the Sorbonne in France. . . .

It was quite an experience for us at the university. We didn't have any money. So we put on programs for various organizations. Molly was a dancer, and I talked about some of the Indian culture in general.

I used to attend quite regularly the various programs at International House and met many students. The committee woman there took it upon herself to contact Dr. Speck to ask if she could offer these two Indian girls her log house in the country. She'd said she'd be very happy to have us if we wanted to spend some time in the log house in the country. Through the years I was more or less used to that sort of thing. For the most part, I found it amusing. It didn't irritate me to that extent.

At International House, there would be programs, weekly international groups, and Friday night dinner and dances and "Around the World in Eighty Minutes," a program to raise money for International House.

On one occasion our group of performers from International House was at

Gladys at the University of Pennsylvania, 1919.

this hotel ready to go on. One of the women attendants in the hotel rooms there, she was looking around at the different girls who were putting on their costumes to be ready for their appearance.

She stopped and looked at me and said, "What are you?"

I said, "American Indian, Mohegan Indian."

"Well," she said, "you don't look like an Indian, you don't talk like an Indian, and that's not an Indian dress."

So I had no comment.

At International House, so many students had read James Fenimore Cooper's *Last of the Mohicans* and so to have a Mohegan or Mohican show up was unheard of. I had not read Cooper's book so I thought I'd better gaze through it. It was difficult for some to understand why my tribal name, Mohegan, was spelled so differently. So I used to have to do some explaining.

Gladys supported much of Speck's work because she believed he was more open-minded than most scholars of his day. However, she met many decidedly narrower minds at the Speck home in Swarthmore, Pennsylvania. Dinner guests there included such well-known academicians as Alfred Kroeber, Clark Wissler, and Franz Boas. Having spent her childhood learning Indian culture, Gladys found herself confronting analysis of her people by men whose understanding was severely limited. Nonetheless, she respected the standing they held within *their* world, and some of them even appreciated hers:

It was quite an exciting place to be. There was one occasion when the American Anthropological Association was having its meeting in Philadelphia. One of my friends—she and I used to travel back and forth from Swarthmore— she was taking some work in the department—so Dorothy and I were up in the far end of the room. I don't remember what we were working on. But Dr. Speck's was a fairly large-size office. Dr. Irving Hallowell had another room downstairs. So the door opened, and in came Clark Wissler, Dr. Alfred Kroeber, Dr. Franz Boas. All celebrities coming in. It was quite exciting.

On another occasion ... Dr. Boas—you know he was referred to as the Father of Anthropology—he was in Philadelphia, and I had been working with him. At that time he was giving a series of talks at Bryn Mawr, and so several of us attended a couple of his lectures. Dr. Speck would have been one of his students. Franz Boas gave me a necklace out of walrus tusk that came from way up in the Hudson Bay area.

CHAPTER 11

MISSING PIECES

In that place there was nothing at all times above the earth. At first
forever lost in space the Great Manitou was. Then on the earth was
an extended fog, and there the Great Manitou was. He made all the
land and the sky. He made the sun, the moon, and the stars. He
made them all move evenly. Then the wind blew violently, and it
cleared, and the water flowed off far and strong. And groups of
islands grew newly and there remained. All beings were then
friendly. Truly the Great Manitou was active and kindly.

—Delaware creation story recited to Gladys by WITAPONOXWE
(Walks with Daylight)

In the spring of 1930, as Gladys walked her path, she stumbled upon her
Lenni Lenape (Delaware) roots. Her new trail guide was to be Witaponoxwe,
a Delaware medicine man, whose well-chosen name meant Walks with
Daylight. The Mohegans were once one of three original Lenni Lenape clans,
which included turtles, turkeys, and wolves. As the wolf group, Mohegans
had migrated east, away from the other two clans. The spirits showed Gladys
that it was time to renew that old acquaintance.

Under the guidance of Witaponoxwe, Gladys relearned old stories, shared
experiences of dream visions, and explored hidden knowledge of medicine
plants. Many of the Delaware customs were quite similar to those of the
Mohegans. But the Delaware had also migrated long ago, to the Southwest,
to Oklahoma, and the climate changes had altered some of their plant us-
ages. For example, the Mohegans carried muskrat root to prevent disease,

Witaponoxwe (Walks with Daylight), a Lenni Lenape (Delaware) medicine man, circa 1900.

and the Delaware took up peyote for that same purpose. However, both used yokeag and prepared it in similar fashion.

Elders had taught both Gladys and Witaponoxwe that there was more to healing than simply administering herbal remedies. Personal gain and trickery could not enter medicine practices. Knowing that illness was the fault of bad spirits, they learned that failure to do ceremonies of thanksgiving and denial of the laws of nature enticed negative beings.

Only good spirits brought good medicine, and those same good spirits had arranged for their meeting. These two medicine folks believed in the Little People and associated them with good spirits. In the Mohegan language a single little person is a *Makiawis,* and in the Delaware, a *Matekanis.*

One day there came a person, and the person was James Webber, known as Witaponoxwe, which means Walks with Daylight. Dr. Speck's wish was to continue research on the Delaware, and this person connected with the Pennsylvania Museum and Historical Commission was to enable him and his students to continue the research. Dr. Speck remarked that "about that time In walked Witaponoxwe." He said, "The Lord sent Witaponoxwe." So it was through that grant from the Historical Commission that I conducted my work.

He, Witaponoxwe, was of fairly sturdy build, and you would immediately say that he was of the "old Indian type" . . . Indian skin, hair, and eyes. He was quiet, very good natured (occasionally he would add a bit of humor), but a very serious-type person.

Dr. Speck was interested in recording about the Delaware Big House Ceremony and minor ceremonies, and my interest was largely in the folk medicine. Another student I worked with—he chose to research the peyote cult. So Witaponoxwe was a medicine man, and we had many interesting sessions while he would dictate the information about the Big House. There would be times when I would question him about the use of plants and the Delaware methods of curing. There were probably not too many differences in the plants we discussed, and the stories about the grandfathers: False Face

Medicine Man and Turtle. He mentioned that they are referred to as grandfathers because they are very old and know a great deal.

Comparing Delaware Medicine Man Witaponoxwe's herbal healing with that of Mohegans: there were, among the Delaware, more survivals of different practices that individuals might have had than I would have run across, because we were fewer in number than the Oklahoma Delawares. The Mohegan would have had non-Indian doctors at a very early time. As late as 1860, thereabouts, a non-Indian doctor rode through Mohegan country on horseback once a year. If you had illnesses at other times, you had to resort to herbal cures. Sometimes there were medicines for colds such as boneset tea. Onions were used a great deal in treating colds. The onion syrup didn't taste very good, but it proved to be effective in many cases. I don't recall that any of our grandmothers and aunts had any secret formula that probably went back to a much earlier period. I don't know to what extent that existed in the Oklahoma and Canadian Delawares.

But at that time, the medicine women at Mohegan didn't have much business in the field of treating the Mohegan and their non-Indian neighbors, although sometimes they were called in to treat the non-Indians in the community.

After college, Gladys built upon the teachings of Witaponoxwe by visiting the Nanticoke Tribe of Virginia and the Cayuga of Ontario. Just as the Mohegans were members of the Delaware's Wolf Clan, the Nanticoke and a few Cayuga were also offshoots of that same Delaware group. However, Gladys found that Nanticoke medicine was so powerful that it sometimes passed over into dangerous areas. She reminded herself of her grandmothers' prohibitions and stayed especially focused on good medicine:

I first visited with the Nanticoke at Thanksgiving time in 1921, thereabouts. After that, I traveled there quite regularly until about 1931. Branches of the Delaware and Nanticoke had both migrated to live among the Six Nations in

1735, at the invitation of the Cayuga. Parts of both groups still inhabited southeastern Pennsylvania. My work among the Nanticoke included studying with the elders. I worked with Wyniaco (Chief Russell Clark) and his wife, Florence Drain Clark, and their son Ferdinand; the Wright brothers—Warren, Elwood, and Walter; and Willie and Annie Harmon and their daughter Janie; Lincoln and Patia Harmon; Levin Street; Mrs. Bumberry; and Howard and Eliza Johnson. At Thanksgiving in 1921, we in the anthropology department went to visit the elders of the Nanticoke Tribe in Indian River Hundred, Sussex County, Delaware. About a dozen or fifteen people were in our group—students and faculty. They, the Nanticoke, had simple ceremonials. We had meetings with families in the community. I had learned from the Delaware that the Nanticoke had an old tradition that involved rituals of courtship. Some of those rituals remained. For example, to attract a mate, you throw a ball of yarn out the window and say, "I wind my yarn, who'll wind agin me?" Whoever picks it up will marry you. But some of their other practices were considered to be a tricky form of medicine.

There were a number of the faculty members, and it was kind of like a big family. Even when we would go on the trips that I mentioned, it would be a number of assistants and their wives and students on vacation periods, even from other colleges. Harvard and Tufts would be in the group that would go—kind of strange arrangements.

In 1931, Gladys visited the Cayuga on the Grand River Reserve in Brant County, Ontario. She found out that some Delaware and Nanticoke people had migrated north to join the Cayuga in the early eighteenth century. A few native Canadian elders remembered that old connection, and Gladys investigated that link with Martha Peters Hill, Nicholas Powless, Joseph Montour, John Lickers, and Walter Moses. She noted several differences between the Canadian Delaware and Witaponoxwe's people. For instance, the Canadian Delaware would not use boneset as a medicine, considering it so potent as to be dangerous. Among the Mohegans and Oklahoma Delaware, boneset was one of the most highly regarded herbs. Still, the Midwinter Longhouse was a tradition common to Cayuga, Delaware, and Mohegans alike.

Gladys's elders taught that, in an everyday *quanukamuk* (longhouse), men and women sat on opposite sides. The size of that long, rounded structure was proported to have been as large as eighty feet. The Midwinter Longhouse was the cold weather ceremonial counterpart of the Mohegans' summer Wigwam festival. To honor and remember that practice, Gladys's brother Harold built a longhouse behind the Tantaquidgeon home in the winter of 1931. At Cayuga, Gladys was first introduced to the ancient winter game of snow snakes. That tribe gave her a pair to take home and treasure.

We attended the winter festival of the Cayuga in the longhouse. That was most impressive. I felt I was out to learn. We had a friend who had been down to the university, and he was Cayuga and told us quite a good deal. There were reports about some of the ceremonials, that we couldn't take notes in the longhouse. This was in January. The big longhouse seats were arranged on either side. On one end would be the chiefs, and women on one side and the boys with their mothers, until about the age of puberty. It was most impressive seeing them bring in the fire, and there were hours of speeches and various ceremonials and food. Certain Indian soup was served. . . .

One day, it was announced that one of the chiefs had died, and that meant that they had to install a man to fill that office immediately. Different rituals had to be stopped, and they had the installation of the new chief. What was very interesting, too, was how they used wampum strings. They explained to us that if the dark beads predominate those beads indicate bad news. Our informant explained to us the way they used these belts and strings: "If a white man gives a talk he writes out his notes. We, in the longhouse—wampum tells us what to say next."

This was all after I met Witaponoxwe, because I wanted to do research to tie in with the Oklahoma Delaware. Some of the Delaware were in Canada and in Ontario. Some were on the East Coast, and it was a small band that had veered off to the North and found themselves over with the Cayuga in Oshwekun, Ontario.

Chief Joseph Montour told me the story of how his band of Delawares had come to contact with the Cayuga Six Nations. He said his people had run out of food, and so the Cayuga chief said they could stay overnight and they would give them breakfast. He laughed and said, "We've been here 150 years."

So that was my contact with the Canadian Delaware.

Gladys was rapidly learning the extended nature of her Indian family. Her fieldwork also included the Naskapi, a group related to the Mohegan as a northern Algonquian branch. In 1929, when she visited them at Lake St. John, Canada, she found these people true to their ancient ways. Those Caribou hunters of the frigid north were the subject of much early twentieth-century "salvage anthropology." Not yet tainted by reliance on European trade goods, they showed Gladys the old ways of parfleche and gave her a painted caribou skin shirt. Other gifts included snowshoes and instructions in loving animal care, which involved the making of small moccasins for sled dogs. She also witnessed some very old medicine for divining the caribou hunt. In that ceremony, burnt cracklings of caribou scapula suggested the direction for hunters to follow. What most surprised Gladys was that even far away from home the "moccasin telegraph" had spread word of her Mohegan people.

In 1931 I obtained the toboggan, snowshoes, and moose skin moccasins that you see at the museum. They always remind me of my visit to the Montagnais Naskapi settlement of Lake St. John, Province of Quebec, Canada.

I was visiting the Lake St. John group with Dr. Speck and his wife. We had for a number of years worked with . . . groups in that area. The Lake St. John group is about two hundred miles north of the city of Quebec, and it's one of the smaller of the bands of the Montagnais Naskapi. It was very exciting, and I think that my first impression was that there were a number of families living in a canvas tent in the cold of winter. They obtained these tents from the Hudson's Bay trading post.

They are hunters—they live hunting caribou. It was December, and the younger men and their families were out hunting and trapping, leaving only the elderly and mothers with young children in the village. Upon entering the tent, we observed the seating custom. The host and his wife were at the rear, and Dr. Speck, his wife, and myself, we seated ourselves accordingly. Men were on one side and women on the opposite side. As customary, there is a period of silence, and then the host starts the conversation. The silence lasted a little longer than usual, and I wondered why. I wondered if I had offended. Finally our host asked Dr. Speck if I was a Mohawk, but they were very cordial when they heard Mahikanni (Naskapi for Mohegan). He knew Mahikanni were kin. So the word spread around that I needed snowshoes, and I needed moccasins. So I was measured for snowshoes and moccasins. It happened very suddenly, and later in the day they had a pair of moccasins for me. Another gift from the Naskapi was the ivory necklace that I wear with my regalia. The Naskapi men carve sections out of walrus tusks, and the women string them.

During that time I studied medicine plants with Mr. and Mrs. Simon Tcelnic, Anastasie Basil, David Basil, Klarence Tcelnic, and Marie and Ambrose Pikutlahigen. They all said they had heard of a place called Boston to the south, and they called us Bostomeo—Boston People.

CHAPTER 12

FOR MOSHUP AND GRANNY

Referred to in a most reverential way by the natives as Granny
Squannit, she has the appearance of a little old woman. . . . She was
the giver of many blessings to her people. All that she asked of
them in return for the many hours which she bestowed upon them
was an offering of food.

—GLADYS TANTAQUIDGEON, recording Wampanoag beliefs

Gladys's fieldwork included living with her Gay Head and Mashpee
Wampanoag "cousins" in Massachusetts off and on during the late 1920s
and early 1930s. Her nanus had mentioned that Moshup had left his footprints in Wampanoag territory. So Gladys hoped to exchange information
on that giant, the Little People, and other somewhat concealed entities.

Choosing to believe in the Little People had been Gladys's first step onto
the medicine trail. The Wampanoags offered her the opportunity to return
that gift of the Little People. Well aware that showing overt appreciation of
them could destroy her scholarly career, her hope was nonetheless to undo
the patronizing stories fashionable among scholars of her day.

In 1929, the Wampanoag elders Eben Queppish and Emma Mitchell
Safford gave Gladys offering baskets for Granny Squannit, leader of the Little
People. Along with those baskets, they shared many stories about the be-
nevolent Granny and about beings of a *darker* nature: Pagak, a human skel-
eton that moves as fast as it thinks; and the *Memegwessi,* small hairy mon-
keylike creatures with ugly faces who paddle rough canoes and steal fish.

The elders revealed light and dark spirit beings that Gladys had never before imagined. In spite of those valuable new introductions, she chose to stay focused on Granny and on trying to undo outsider misunderstandings. For example, the well-known colonial leader Roger Williams had wrongly called Granny "The Woman's God" and referred to her Indian people as "savages and barbarians."[21] But the Wampanoags spoke of her lovingly as having hair that looked like a haystack and tiny toenails made of the golden shells along the beaches. Granny also had two diamond-shaped eyes and a third, central spirit eye.

At Mohegan many of the older Indian men and women regarded their knowledge and expertise in their respective skills as personal property. For example, if the art of healing was revealed to a boy or girl at the age of puberty, that spiritual gift must be guarded by the person to whom it was given. Likewise certain skills in crafts would be passed on to certain individuals. In the case of a medicine man or woman, many never shared their knowledge with anyone.

So when I visited Mashpee on Cape Cod in the summer in search of information on folk medicine and legends, I was told that the only one left who had such knowledge was Eben Queppish. It was also stated that he was a basket maker but would not talk to anyone. That was discouraging news for me.

However, that evening after supper I journeyed down to the general store and post office with the niece and nephew of the Mashpee family where I was boarding. There the Indians and non-Indians gathered to pick up the mail and share accounts of the day's activities.

About the fourth evening, one of my Mashpee friends told me that Eben wished to meet me. He had heard that my father made baskets, so we talked basketry materials, different types, and weaves. He asked me if I knew the hexagonal or openwork weave, and when I seemed a little vague about that particular weave, he volunteered to teach me. Eben had the ash splints and said that he would come to the home where I was boarding. So in a few days Eben appeared, and I began my lessons in making a special type of basket. He explained that Little People lived in the woods and along the beaches and that in early times it was customary for groups going out to gather food plants, herbs for medicine, fishing, or hunting, to put some corn bread and meat in a small basket and leave it for the Little People. He added, "That was for good luck." Also while he made baskets, Eben told me about some herbal remedies as well as legends.

He was a conservative and lamented the fact that so much of the early culture of our people in southern New England had disappeared. When I returned to Mashpee the following year, Eben had passed away. The two offering baskets in our collection were made during my pleasant hours with this fine Mashpee gentleman.[22]

To defend the Little People, Gladys published several remarkable articles, but what she wrote about their leader in unpublished form is most inspiring. Her story "Granny Squannit's Garden" was too high-minded for 1930s academia. The tale involved obtaining herbal cures through ritual and prayer to a native entity. Her serious advocacy of either that form of medicine or that form of religion would have drawn scorn and mockery from the scholars of her generation. Now that such ancient elemental wisdom is nearly gone, twenty-first-century scholars desperately seek it.

To contact Granny Squannit, a person concentrates on the thing which he wants, and in due time the wish is granted.

Granny gave to the Indians the knowledge of medicinal properties found in certain plants and also knowledge of how to prepare roots for use in curing certain diseases. The essential idea involved is embodied in the principle of making offerings for the purpose of sharing her blessings. The origin of plant foods and medicines is not attributed to her. She performs the function of allotting to humans a share of her domain of blessings. Granny exercises beneficent care not only for the material needs of the Indians but for their spiritual requirements. She shows solicitude by answering the wish or supplication of the doctor, provided he remembers the obligation of offering her a gift to show his devout attitude toward her. . . . To obtain this valuable information the medicine man or woman would proceed as follows:

He is called upon to treat an individual. He diagnoses the case and perhaps finds that the plant required in making the medicine to be administered is a rare one. Or he may be baffled and not have any clue to the right medicine to use. He must rely on Granny Squannit. He must be in earnest and put all else out of his mind. An offering of food is prepared—some cornbread or other dainty morsels—either in a small bag or arranged on a plate. In some instances they offered wine. They took this to where . . . she might find it and placed it on a tree stump or placed it on the ground, protected by leaves and branches. The offering was usually placed at night, and the next day the herb seeker returned to the spot to find several fine specimens of the desired plant growing in what they call Granny Squannit's Garden. Those plants were not plucked, but others of the same species were sought. My informants have given most detailed accounts of how the Indian doctors appealed to Granny Squannit and the miraculous cures which they effected. Several of the persons interviewed said that they had seen Granny Squannit; others believe her to be an invisible spirit. It is said she disappeared because the people did not bring her offerings and generally disregarded her existence.

Gladys's research focused on the benefits of native healing at a time when the dominant American culture disdained the treatments of Indian medicine men and women. Colonial missionaries branded them devils, witches, sorcerers, and witch doctors. Removing those long-standing word blocks and dispelling the prejudice, Gladys focused on the need to unveil the good in Indian medicine. Her enlightening trek from Indian country to white academia and back again imbued her work with a rare perspective. Gladys compared the Mohegan pantheon to its counterparts among related tribes

(like the Wampanoag). Then, she contrasted her findings with the interpretations assigned by non-Indian scholars.

Granny and her husband, Moshup, were well-recorded culture heros to
many indigenous peoples. But Gladys found that they were long considered villains by the missionaries and fantasies by academicians like Speck.
The Wampanoags, for example, knew that whales were Moshup's special
creatures and that skate egg cases were his pocketbooks—not "Devil's pocketbooks" as the old-time missionaries used to say. In recording a
Wampanoag Moshup story Gladys showed how non-Indian perspective had
permeated but not destroyed Indian belief.

After the coming of the white men or *watacoma–og* (men with coats), the
destiny of Moshup, the good spirit of Martha's Vineyard was about to be
fulfilled. He told them, his simple subjects, that as the light had come among
them and as he belonged to the Kingdom of Darkness, he must take his leave;
which to their great sorrow he accordingly did and has never been heard of
since.[23]

Among the Wampanoags, Gladys heard far more about Moshup than at
Mohegan, since she was living directly on the seacoast with people for
whom whaling and seafaring were not limited to a few elders' memories.

In Gay Head, we lived with the Ryan family. Then, one of the members was
keeper of the Gay Head light. While I was there, I heard about the Little
People and their giant counterparts in casual references to weather. Some of
the family might come in and say, "Well, Moshup and Granny must be
fighting, because the sea is pretty rough."

Moshup lived on the extreme end of Gay Head, and some said he had only
one eye in the middle of his forehead. Little Granny—in the case of the Gay
Head—they said she lived along the shore, among the rocks. You weren't
supposed to see her. But they had the same custom of leaving offerings for

her as we do at Mohegan. One informant said you weren't supposed to see Granny and Moshup because they were invisible.

Tamson Weeks and Esther Howossowee, those two women of the Gay Head, taught Rachel Ryan a great deal about the use of plants and the characters in folklore. They also spoke of Granny Squannit and Moshup. They said Moshup was powerful and could capture whales. He could also help young lovers find happiness.

Having cared well for their old stories, the Wampanoags inspired Gladys to create a place where everyone would hear and learn to respect such tales of old New England. In 1930, she spoke with her father, John, and her brother Harold about creating that dream.

Offering baskets for the Makiawisug (Little People) given to Gladys in the 1920s by the Wampanoags Eben Queppish and Emma Mitchell Safford.

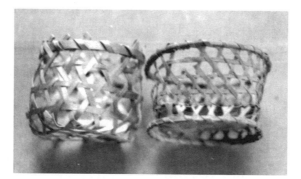

CHAPTER 13

TANTAQUIDGEON MUSEUM

When the white man talks about our culture, he's skating on thin
ice; when you talk about our culture, you're skating on the thick
ice. Stand tall and firm on the thick ice.

—HAROLD TANTAQUIDGEON

Gladys chose to record her journeys to other eastern tribes by collecting
and cataloguing their treasured gifts. To anthropologists, those gifts were
mere artifacts. Gladys greeted them as living treasures. She knew that in-
troducing these treasures to the world could reveal the true stories of Indian people. If visitors saw Mohegan and Wampanoag offering baskets for
the Little People, Gladys would have an opportunity to tell them the truth
about Granny and her husband, Moshup. This clarification of the record
was one of the inspirations behind creating Tantaquidgeon Museum atop
Mohegan Hill. Gladys cofounded that institution in 1931 with her brother
Harold and father, John.

The stories told about artifacts and Mohegan magical beliefs at
Tantaquidgeon Museum would be the stories told by the Indians themselves. The creation of that museum offered a heavy dose of good medicine
to the Mohegans. Now when non-Indians asked questions about their heritage, Mohegans no longer sent them to a non-Indian institution for sec-
ondhand answers. At Tantaquidgeon Museum, no condescending curator
would make disparaging remarks about the primitive, prehistoric, or su-
perstitious nature of Indians. The stories told would be personal tales de-
signed to share the beauty of aboriginal truths.

At the height of the Great Depression, John Tantaquidgeon took a leap of faith and built that museum. He was a quiet wood-carver and basketmaker to whom money meant nothing. Blind in one eye, he walked only on crutches and canes. His life found its truest meaning in turning maple trees into ladles and oak trees into splint baskets. The only thing more dear to him was having a museum to preserve those things and the objects made by other Indian people. His own good spirits guided the museum project and blessed it on opening day.

On the evening the museum opened, the Tantaquidgeon family took out its special black china and held a dinner inside the museum with their friends. Included among them were the anthropologist Frank Speck, Chief Matahga of the Mohegans, and other local tribal leaders, such as Chief Silver Star of the Pequots, and Medicine Man Pine Tree of the Narragansetts. This assemblage included dreamers who saw in the Tantaquidgeon family's achievement a great hope for the future. Today the Tantaquidgeon Museum is the oldest Indian owned and operated museum in America.

Father and brother Harold built the little stone original museum that was begun in 1930 and completed and opened in 1931. The purpose of this little stone room was to house our collection of various artifacts that had been made and used by our people and were scattered about our living quarters here and there so that not only our own people could enjoy them but others as well.

When brother Harold was available and around, then he would be "on deck" to give tours, and when I was here, why, I would be there to take care of visitors. Sometimes it was necessary for both of us to be.

Father was disabled at the time, and he had to use a cane, and he was blind in one eye. But according to what my brother said, I guess he handled every one of the granite fieldstones used in the construction of that building. If one seemed to be just a little bit out of place, he had to see that it was taken care of. It was a family affair, and Dr. Speck and his family were very supportive.

When it was finally completed, members of the community and other Mohegans brought in things to put on display.

From the beginning, Tantaquidgeon Museum was to be the place where we
keep Mohegan treasures. The woodland section of the museum is home. Some
artifacts are very old, and some were made recently. Family treasures are there,
such as the ancient mortar and pestle used by many generations. . . . certain
baskets, bowls of maple wood, as well as scoops, beaded purses, and a belt
given to me by my great-aunt Fidelia Hoscott Fielding, known as Flying Bird.
This belt is an important part of my ceremonial dress. It had belonged to
Martha Uncas, Fidelia's grandmother and was probably made in the late
1700s. The simple designs are on black velvet. The center front and back
designs are variations of the symbol of four—four winds or four directions.
On either side of the central figures are the sacred tree symbols growing
from the earth to the sky.

One small ash splint basket circa 1840—about four by four by four inches,
open or hexagonal—we were told was used as an offering basket in which
meat and corn bread were placed and left in the woods for the Little People.
The battered broken old oak splint basket rescued by my sister and brother-
in-law when they purchased the Samson Occum house (home of the first
ordained Mohegan Indian minister) was made by Jerome Bohema, a full-
blood Mohegan who taught my father, John Tantaquidgeon, the skills of preparing the wood splints and the weaving techniques. My father took this
broken basket and repaired it. It now hangs in Tantaquidgeon Museum as a
reminder of the work of two Mohegan basket makers. John Tantaquidgeon
made baskets until 1934, when he was obliged to cease due to failing eyesight.
Examples of his basketry and other woodwork date back to 1888. Several of
his beautiful scoops, spoons, and ladles of maple wood bear dates in the early
1930s. There are also some of his axe and hammer handles of hickory and
white oak. One maple bowl made by my father about 1930 has delicate leaf
carvings done by my brother Harold Tantaquidgeon.

The oldest bows and arrows (around 1879) on display are made of black ash and were made by Henry Mathews, affectionately referred to as Wegun meaning Good. The two arrows with blunt ends were used to stun small animals. Nearby is a bow with three arrows made by his grandson, Roscoe Skeesucks. On either end of the bow is a face painted half red and half black symbolizing day and night or life and death. The three arrows have stone, bone, and steel points. There are other bows which were made by John and Harold Tantaquidgeon and Skeesucks.

Skeesucks also made two stirring paddles, "puddin' sticks," about a foot long. They have carved handles, one with turtles and the other with two faces. He also made a basket of birch bark, which has a border decoration of shells and trade beads.

Mercy Ann Nonesuch Mathews (affectionately known to us as Grandma Mathews) did some beadwork, and we have several small pouches and a needle case as examples of her skill. Also a reversible doll, or two-headed doll, if you will. This doll was made for my grandmother Fielding about 1860. There are baskets, spoons, scoops, and a bow and arrow made by her son Charles Mathews. Her husband, Henry, around 1869 made wood carvings, birch bark baskets, bows and arrows. Roscoe Skeesucks was her grandson.

These are some of the things I treasure most at the museum.[24]

Hilltop society had a new focal point once the museum opened. Community gatherings were no longer limited to Mohegan Church or Shantok. Gladys held Indian Nights, when dinner and a lecture cost fifty cents. Included were homemade clear broth clam chowder, ice cream sprinkled with yokeag, cake, and coffee. These outdoor suppers featured guest speakers, like Gladys's friend Ta-de-win from the *Christian Science Monitor.* The museum had become a sort of longhouse or gathering lodge for the Mohegans. But the course of Gladys's trail would not let her remain at home for long.

Tantaquidgcon Museum in the 1930s. Note the diamond on the chimney and the mortar and pestle in front.

CHAPTER 14

QUALIFYING TRIALS

The Mohegans chose to end their reservation in the 1860s due to
the corrupt practices of their government overseers.

—GLADYS TANTAQUIDGEON

In 1934, the United States Congress passed the Wheeler-Howard Act, popu-
larly known as the Indian Reorganization Act. The policies it set forth were
those of the new commissioner of Indian affairs, John Collier, a reformer
whose agenda would return self-government to Indian nations. Although
the new law encouraged tribes to draft American-style constitutions, which
eroded the authority of traditional leaders like chiefs and medicine people,
it did represent a positive approach to American Indian sovereignty, and it
also provided funding for Indian education. The Indian Reorganization Act
was controversial then, and is still hotly debated among Indians today, but
Gladys and others hoped that it would help Indian people. Offered a government job under the new law, she was to determine scholarship eligibil-
ity among northeastern Indians. To qualify, individuals had to be at least
one-quarter Indian. Mindful that her grandmothers had mistrusted government overseers in the midnineteenth century and that "Feds" had tried
to remove Mohegans from the hill in the 1830s, Gladys feared becoming
the enemy. She was relieved to receive wonderful treatment from Governor Joseph Nichols of the Passamaquoddy Tribe as well as the Penobscot
people, who donated a birch bark canoe to the Tantaquidgeon Museum.
However, she watched and took note when the Penobscots rebuffed one
condescending government coworker.

I continued working on my folk medicine and folklore, and there came a request for "someone familiar with New England Indians" from the Bureau of Indian Affairs. Dr. Carson Ryan was the head of the Department of Education for the Indian Service at that time, and so Dr. Speck recommended me. That was the beginning of my connection there. That was probably about 1934. I had done my fieldwork in Delaware, Mashpee, and Gay Head before that.

In 1934, I was hired by the federal government to administer benefits to Indians under the Wheeler-Howard Act. Maine was my first stop on that trip in New England. The purpose of it was to visit these different groups in New England to find out if there were any young people who would be interested in applying for educational grants.

Dr. Carson Ryan knew that I had previously been to Penobscot in Maine. On the way there, I met this woman, and she was connected with the BIA. She was "that type" and just so aggressive. When we were talking with a couple of Penobscot Indians, one man was not telling her the truth and just making things up as he went along. Later, he told me that he didn't like the BIA woman and he wasn't going to give her any information that would be helpful.

Gladys was learning that racism can wear many masks: the face of a pushy bureaucrat, of a child who expects certain feats of another, or of a college administrator who segregates students. Her experiences offered her a dingy window onto the world in which her nanus had lived. Outsiders had forbidden her great-aunt Fidelia's speaking her native language and mocked her daily dialogues with spirit beings. Her other great-aunt, Emma, helplessly witnessed construction workers desecrate her ancestors' bodies in Norwich. Emma and Fidelia knew no Mohegan who had yet walked through the fire of racism and come out the other side unsinged. Their recompense would come from Gladys—the woman born to follow the sun.

In 1934, the American South introduced Gladys to a vile form of bigotry generally associated with African Americans: seating at the back of buses.

What is less well known is that similar discrimination occurred against Indians and other people of color. Historians have recorded the bold opposition of African Americans to their racial segregation during the 1960s. It is generally acknowledged that ignorance confined them to the backs of southern buses until Rosa Parks took her lonesome stand. But few people know that in 1934 an Indian woman removed herself from the back of a Virginia bus, thanks to Gladys Tantaquidgeon.

A discrimination case occurred while I was in Washington before I went out West. I had been staying with two young women. One was Seneca, and she was a secretary to Dr. Carson Ryan, and the other was Chippewa. Dr. Ryan knew that I had been to Virginia and was acquainted with some of the Powhatan groups, and he was wanting his secretary to meet some of the tribes, and he asked that I take her down and introduce her to some of the leaders. We had to go by bus part way to Chickahominy, and when we boarded the bus I was kind of tired and took a seat. My friend and coworker sat behind me, and I sort of dozed slightly, and when I turned to speak to her she wasn't there in the seat behind me, because the driver had asked her to move to the rear of the bus. So I turned and motioned to her to come back—which she did. I went forward to the bus driver and got my ID card and mentioned to him that he made a mistake. He said he didn't mean any harm, and I told him it was quite serious because we were both American Indian.

Such trials along her life trail made Gladys stronger and her good medicine more potent than before. As the intensity of her challenges increased, she was drawn farther into the world of the spirit. Little by little, her choices broke her connections to the physical world. Constant traveling had denied her friends, a husband, and children. As if to solidify her break with the material world, in 1935 *Wejut Mundo*, the Fire Spirit, told her it was time to move on.

That year, the federal government was shuffling Indians under the new

A conference of Indian service officials, Denver, 1939. Gladys is in the third row, second from left. John Collier is in the first row, third from left.

Indian Reorganization Act. That flurry provoked a desperate search for well-schooled natives to work on western reservations slated for reorganization. Her educational background and multitribal experience made Gladys an obvious choice for a position as a federal Native American community worker.

In 1934, I met with Commissioner of Indian Affairs John Collier in his Washington, D.C., office. That was really a scary occasion. I had been through the capitol city and seen some of the sights. To actually be interviewed for this position was a little bit breathtaking.

However Mr. Collier was a very quiet unassuming individual, and it went very well. He mentioned to me that this assignment on the Yangton Sioux Reservation was one of the more difficult in Indian service. He explained to me that the Yangton Sioux had sold some of their land and had been paid a considerable amount of money and with that money had built modern . . . dwellings and had bought some modern clothing. That was due to the fact that, as soon as the word had spread around that these people sold the land and had all this money to spend, there were those who made haste to go to the reservation and interest them . . . in buying many things which they didn't need. Of course the clothing and other things didn't last too long, and by this time many of them were destitute. By this time homes needed repair. So the Yangton Sioux tribal members were in great need.

The whole program of self-government for Indian tribes was beginning. Mr. Collier said he wanted the Indians to help themselves. I felt I was there not to tell the people what to do, but to work with them in a way that would enable them to desire better living quarters and better schools.

After my interview with Commissioner Collier, I was staying a few days in Washington being interviewed. I was advised by the head of the Social Services Department Education Division that I had received a telegram. Our home had burned. So the office granted me five days leave so I could go home. My clothing, books, and material were all packed, ready to be shipped out, and it was all burned.

PART III

WESTERN TRAIL

CHAPTER 15

AMONG THE LAKOTA SIOUX

In the past, things Indian were rather frowned upon, and every effort was made to try to have these people forget as much of their culture as possible: their language, ceremonies, tribal customs. Part of our work . . . was to undo that.

—Comments on the Lakota Sioux, by GLADYS TANTAQUIDGEON

In the midnineteenth century, the United States government took the sacred lands of the Black Hills from the Lakota Nation, then called Sioux, a corruption of an Ojibway Indian term for enemy. From those lands come the *paha sapa* red clay that the Lakotas used to create beautiful pottery painted with such ancient symbols as the diamond, representing the eye of the Great Spirit, and peaked triangles, signifying pathways across mountain ranges. The Badlands form much of the remaining Lakota territory. The names of reservation communities—No Water, Bad Wound, No Flesh, Little Wound, and Loneman—tell of hardship and suffering. Yet, physical hardship alone could not crush the Lakota. Thus, federal Indian agents also attempted to break the connection between Sioux life and afterlife: denial of Lakota treaty claims to the Black Hills damaged that link between the Trail of Life and the Beautiful White Path. Like Mohegan Hill, the Black Hills hold the spirit of the Indian nation.[25]

When Gladys visited the Sioux people in the 1930s, symptoms of broken life trails were everywhere. Decades of suppression of language, ceremony, government, and medicine had shredded the fabric of the native world. Similar rapes of traditions had taken place at Mohegan and throughout East Coast Indian country for centuries before the Sioux met a white man.

Gladys's nanus remembered those violations, and each dealt with her recollections uniquely. Fidelia Fielding withdrew from the world of people into the world of the spirit. Emma Baker confronted white legislators at the state capitol in Hartford. Mercy Ann Nonesuch Mathews resisted, saying, "Just because they declare me extinct that does not make me extinct." Fidelia, Emma, and Mercy had placed at least one foot outside the tunnel of despair that had trapped their ancestors. Gladys would forge beyond them. Her trail of life would include an era of Mohegan rejuvenation.

Gladys spent most of her time among the Lakota on the Pine Ridge and Rosebud reservations (which adjoin in south central South Dakota) and the Santee and Yankton Sioux reservations (which are smaller and farther east). Each reservation represents a different tribal group within the larger Lakota Nation. Although Lakota territory is vast, little land is suited to agriculture. Growing corn was very difficult on the reservations. Because the Lakotas, like the Mohegans, believe that corn feeds the body and the spirit, crop failure proved dually lethal:

It was pretty rough to earn a living. I suppose if the corn fields were flourishing it might be possible to earn a living. On one occasion I came back from the Pine Ridge reservation, and just in a few days the grasshoppers and crickets had the corn stalks as bare as your fingers, and what amazed me was that the people would accept that and start all over again. There really wasn't much they could do.

Death visited the Lakota often. In recounting the tragedies she witnessed, Gladys remembered two mourning dolls, one a man and one a woman, each with cropped hair. The Yankton Sioux gave her these extraordinarily crafted figures. Each represented a loved one who had passed on and who required one year of formal mourning.

There was one man who evidently didn't use his food for the family (which was supposedly enough to last a week or ten days). So this one man—

evidently he had a little celebration and used up all the food in one after-noon or night. Once there was an investigation when word got around that someone had starved to death. There had been a little gathering at his home, and his son had made puppy stew. Whether it didn't agree with the elderly man, I don't know. But there was an investigation from Washington. A man came to my office and asked about this man and wanted to see what food had been issued. But he saw that food had been issued to him regularly . . . sugar, butter, cheese, and sometimes meat. But the report was . . . that an Indian had starved to death for lack of food. So when two other social workers and myself had to have our travel authorities reviewed . . . had to go to the office of field operations. . . . the commissioner was signing these documents, and he—with kind of a stressed look—said, "Which one of you young ladies is responsible for allowing the man on the reservation to starve to death?"

So I very shyly said, "I'm the one, sir."

He laughed and said, "Well, we have these reports come in, and we under-stand the situation there," and he said, "Just go back to your headquarters and do the best you can."

There was another occasion when this child, probably seven or eight months old, had died, and the word had been passed around that it was due to infantile paralysis or some other contagious disease. No one wanted to touch the baby, and there was no hospital on the reservation. The contract physician had pronounced the baby dead, and one of the police officers asked me to go into the family house. I dressed the baby for burial, and while I did this I noticed injury to the head and shoulders.

From 1935 to 1937, Gladys lived with Sioux people on various reserva-tions. She was aware that, before the Indian Reorganization Act of 1934, the government had instructed its workers to convert those Indians to Euro-American lifeways. Gladys knew that the state of Connecticut had given similar instructions to Mohegan overseers in the eighteenth and nineteenth centuries. The quickest way to accomplish assimilation was to bring the Indians to the brink of destitution. Gladys's nanus had described "starving-outs". They told her stories of Uncas's son, Sachem Owaneco (often shortened to Oneco), who had begged for food in the streets of Norwich:

> Oneco, king, his queen doth bring,
> To beg a little food;
> As they go along his friends among
> to try how kind, how good.

Gladys (left) skinning a buffalo at Lakota, 1938.

Some pork, some beef, for their relief,
And if you can't spare bread,
She'll thank you for a pudding, as they go a gooding,
And carry it on her head.[26]

Severe conditions spawned similar humiliations among the Sioux. Destruction of the buffalo and other traditional game animals forced Indians to farm unfarmable land for sustenance. Replacement of traditional tepees with modern houses added winter fuel expenses to already straitened finances during already harsh winters. Fewer ceremonials compounded winter doldrums. Life on the reservations during the 1930s was marginal.

Just think, if I want to purchase anything at a five-and-ten-cent store I must drive 80 miles. And on a warm night we had to drive 15 miles for an ice cream cone. When the superintendent calls a business meeting I drive 180 miles to attend and sometimes return the same day. . . . It's early to bed unless oil lamps or candles are brought out . . . for [though] they generate their own electricity out here, it is turned off at 9:45 p.m. Once a week on Mondays it is turned on in the daytime for washing and again on Wednesday for ironing.[27]

Some fifty years later, she still recalled those years vividly:

I shared government quarters with a teacher in the school that was maybe a quarter of a mile down the road. . . . We had four rooms and a bath with supposedly running water. But in the wintertime it did not run. Everything was frozen tight. We burned soft coal. . . . It doesn't burn through, and so we took turns tending the fire—my coworker and I every other night. . . . We were snowed in most of the time. Pretty difficult for a community worker to make the rounds. The snow drifts would be so high that you would travel through the fields and over the fences. Living conditions on that reservation were pretty bad. I don't believe the family back home had any idea what it was like living there.

The Office of Indian Affairs had appointed a certain number of social workers, and some of us were given the titles of community worker. I went to Anadarko, Oklahoma, and visited a number of families and a number of schools to acquaint me with what my responsibilities might be on the Yankton reservation. Following that, I went to visit the Winnebago agency and also the Santee Sioux, who were under the jurisdiction of the Winnebago agency. Then the next stop was the Rosebud agency, and Yankton was a subagency at Rosebud.

The position of community workers—that was new. It hadn't been very many years, perhaps three or four by the time that I entered the service, that they had community workers. I was assigned to a subagency in the Rosebud jurisdiction. At that time, my immediate supervisor was Ruth Heinman. She was supervisor in charge. . . . Our work was largely interpreting the programs of the BIA, attempting to acquaint the people . . . with some of the changes that had taken place under Commissioner Collier and the Indian Reorganization Act of 1934. . . .

We had staff meetings, once a month, and I would go to the Rosebud agency 180 miles to the west of where I was stationed. We would meet with superintendent of the agency and the heads of the other departments: education, health, and extension. Then occasionally there would be regional meetings. A regional meeting might be held in Denver, Colorado, or Minneapolis, Minnesota.

The denial of fundamental rights was another method intended to break the Sioux. Gladys's experience with segregated seating on buses in the South was a small precursor to the equal rights battles she would face out West. There she learned why her nanus rarely left the safety of Mohegan Hill. Denial of service at eating, drinking, or lodging establishments near the Lakota territory was common.

There would be instances where the Indians would hesitate to speak to or be in the company of government employees, which demonstrates the feeling some Indian people had, not to know whether they would be accepted in a public place. I know one time Flora Go Forth and I had to be at Rosebud, where we were going to demonstrate weaving, and we stopped at a small restaurant. She offered an excuse to go to the store to make some purchase. She told me after that she would be denied service in South Dakota.

CHAPTER 16

FREEING PRISONERS AT LAKOTA

Many objects carry a living spirit.

—GLADYS TANTAQUIDGEON

Like Gladys's Mohegan grandmothers, the Lakota wanted to preserve their native language, keep their natural medicine, restore their old ways of educating the young, and retain the ancient objects of their traditional culture. These objects created by the Sioux, like those made by the Mohegans, were not mere artifacts. They were often sacred ceremonial artworks that reflected the most high-minded spiritual aspects of their society. Lakota people told Gladys that the previous generation had suffered the destruction of many such ceremonial objects by non-Indians. They knew that federal assimilation programs would not succeed as long as those ancient spiritual weapons defended them. Those memories caused many Indians to be wary of Gladys the government worker. She determined to honor the Lakota people and to earn their confidence:

In going about visiting various families, at first it takes a little while for a newcomer to be accepted by the group—which is understandable. When many of the family members and elders, in particular, found that I was of Indian descent, they accepted me and talked to me Indian to Indian as well as Indian to government employee. So I got two sides of every question. Many were hesitant to come into my office. I made it a point to keep my door open. Old-time government offices had grating, like bank tellers, and it was quite some time before some of the elders felt free to come in and sit down and talk.

On one occasion, I visited the home of an elderly couple. I was asking about some of the tribal customs and if anyone in the family did any of the beadwork, quillwork that is customary. After a while, one of the sons opened up a trunk, and he brought out very beautiful pieces of the traditional wearing apparel that had been put aside. He explained that not only his family but others feared that some of those treasures might be taken away from them. . . . Previous workers had done that. It was a policy of the government to discourage the people from making any of these traditional-type garments.

Grounded in traditional Mohegan medicine practices and familiar with those of other eastern tribes, Gladys respected the Sioux commitment to maintaining old medicine ways. However, much of that old medicine was being held hostage along with its ceremonial objects. Old ingredients were difficult to find. Worse yet, even when traditional herbal medicines could be prepared, government workers did not allow western tribes to perform

Southwest/Plains Room of Tantaquidgeon Museum.
Note the tepee with mourning dolls.

the necessary ceremonies for them to take effect. The denial of those ceremonials rendered many cures impotent. Animals like the buffalo, critical in fostering powerful Sioux healing spirits, were nearly gone. Gladys supported Sioux medicine ways, offering the option of Euro-American medicine only as a last resort. She found that replacing even incomplete old native medicine with non-Indian medicine was sometimes poisonous to the Lakota body and spirit:

The Yankton Sioux agency was a small group of employees: an extension worker, a community worker. At that point we didn't have a resident physician and had to take our patients to a hospital that was 150 miles away. We had a temporary doctor that we could call on from about sixteen miles away. So there were many difficult situations where you might have to deal with the sick.

One hot summer day where I was sent to the agency office, one of the men was out mowing in the fields and was bitten by a rattlesnake. I think he opened up a chicken and put some of the intestines on his ankle, but he waited too long probably. Finally the agency superintendent said he would have to go to Rosebud hospital, and this man asked that I be the driver. So here's the hot summer weather and it was four o'clock before we started. We made the hospital, and he was admitted. I had to go on to some other work and came back two days later and stopped at Rosebud, and the patient had died. That was a difficult situation. . . .

It was difficult to explain to some of the elders that they would be given proper care in what they referred to as the white man's hospital. In the case of one mother-to-be, I had arranged for her to go to the hospital to deliver. When it came time, I couldn't find her, and someone told me her grandparents had taken her up in a tepee away from the dwelling where I would find her.

Then on another occasion, the only hospital that offered services for those suffering from TB was in southwest Arizona, and this one young man had all the arrangements made for him . . . so that he could be taken care of in that particular hospital in Arizona. I had barely settled down after making the final arrangements, thinking he had arrived there in Arizona, when in no time he was back on the res. Many of the elders didn't want anything to do with the white man's hospitals and white man's schools. It was a difficult situation for all concerned.

In the early twentieth century, many Lakota children were placed in federal boarding schools far from their reservation homes. That separation of children from their families and communities was another effective way of breaking the tribe's spirit. It was a means of preventing elders from teaching traditional knowledge to the next generation. That system also created a society of parents unprepared for child rearing. Meager incomes made it doubly difficult for Indian parents to keep children at home. Severe problems naturally arose among the Sioux when the Bureau of Indian Affairs phased out that boarding school system in the 1930s. Mindful of the contrast between her own shining home education and her less-pleasant non-Indian schooling, Gladys tried to bring Sioux children back home and to supplement family incomes:

It was then the purpose to build community schools so that the children of these families would attend school near home, rather than be transferred out of state to a boarding school. The agency gave me a folder with fifteen or twenty cases. . . . One of the agency police officers took me around and introduced me to quite a number of families. A common answer to the question about not sending the children away was "We don't know about keeping our children at home. We attended boarding school and our children attended boarding schools. What would we do about food and clothing?"

So we assured them that food and clothing would be taken care of. Our government schools were under the BIA education division. There were schools built in different communities on the reservations, and on one occasion the Office of Education felt that, perhaps, ... the school could be placed on the boundary of two communities. But the Indian members of the groups didn't agree to that. Either the school was in their community or they didn't attend. Some children, if not close enough to the reservation school, would attend the public one-room school. Along with the community schools there were programs for the adults, where they could learn about cooking, sewing. Extension service tried to have cattle, so there would be milk and butter, but the Plains Indians were travelers. So if they wanted to travel to a summer festival or celebration they couldn't take cows along. But somebody thought to try goats, and they worked out pretty well.

One time I went to visit a family for the reason of finding out why a couple of the older children had not been attending school. This would have been a community school not far from their home. So when I went in, there sat just the mother and father, and the mother had a little baby in her arms. I didn't see any other children. So while we were talking—I think they had a total of six children—I saw the hand of one small child poking out from under the bed, and another was in a corner somewhere. So I told them I was not out to punish them or tell other school officials.

Gladys frequently questioned her own actions at Sioux, knowing that however similar the situation was to Mohegan there would forever be differences she could not understand. One Sioux elder affirmed that her hard-wrought decisions were good ones by welcoming her into the community. Acceptance by a ranking Sioux elder connected Gladys to Indian people outside Mohegan and beyond the eastern woodlands. At Sioux, she learned that all of her Indian grandmothers had not yet passed away.

Another woman, named Grandmother White Tallow, I visited quite regularly. She didn't speak any English, and I didn't speak any Sioux. I usually took her some food. She lived in a log house. One day, one of her relatives told me, "Grandmother White Tallow likes you, she calls you granddaughter."

CHAPTER 17

HEALING AND THANKS

Tawbut nee Gunci Mundo, Tawbut nee tukenig kah weous. Mundo Wigo. (Thank you, Great Spirit, thank you for bread and meat. The Creator is good.)

—GLADYS TANTAQUIDGEON

As a BIA community worker in the Lakota territory, Gladys was limited to one region and the confines of social work. In 1938, she decided that she "needed to do more" and readily accepted a position with the newly formed Federal Indian Arts and Crafts Board. Her elders had trained her in the traditional arts of basketry, finger weaving, and beadwork. Those skills would be fine tuned in her new job. A basic problem at Sioux was economics. Therefore, Gladys endorsed bolstering native economies by restoring and selling Indian art. That effort included the rejuvenation of ceremonies related to that art. Gladys had witnessed the powerful effects of reviving the Mohegan Wigwam and preserving the Cayuga Midwinter Longhouse. Through the Indian Arts and Crafts Board, she began a decade's advocacy for the sun dance, rain dance, traditional healing feasts, and the art forms related to such ceremonies. She had seen that the diminution of traditional Indian rituals and artwork created sickness and bad medicine among Indian people. The restoration of native art would be a giant step toward healing a broken circle.

Under the direction of Dr. Rene d'Harnoncourt, her agency work brought her regularly through the Dakotas, Montana, and Wyoming. Gladys taught Indian art, brought native artists to various reservations as teachers, and exhibited the work of Indian artists across the country.

Her new job lessened her contact with indigenous gloom and increased her contact with the shining spiritual side of the American Indian West. Traveling "the museum circuit" from San Francisco to Browning, Montana, Gladys gained museum curatorial experience. Her new skill prepared her to be curator of her family's museum when she returned home in 1947.

Meanwhile her sister Ruth had opened a store called Our Little Shoppe. Ruth sold the work of Indian artists that Gladys sent to her. Many pieces came from Assiniboine, Montana. Moccasins by Mrs. Two Kill sold for about four dollars; belts by Edith Dragonfly, about six. Even in the 1940s, a magnificent pipe and pipe case by Feather Woman brought twenty-five dollars.

The Arts and Crafts Board, at that time it was new and not under the BIA. It was separate under the Department of the Interior. We had a director with headquarters in Washington, D.C.; Rene d'Harnoncourt and his assistant, Ken Disher, were in charge. When I first entered Arts and Crafts, there were only three field workers: one in the Southwest, one in Oklahoma, and I had the northern division of North and South Dakota, Montana, and Wyoming. For example, my work would be with the school principals and staff. I don't recall that any of us were getting very much in salaries at that time.

The exhibits of the Indian Arts and Crafts Board were featured at the San Francisco Exposition of 1939. Fostering Indian arts demanded affluent celebrity promoters, and the First Lady Eleanor Roosevelt and the ventriloquist Edgar Bergen were two such notables. The success of that exhibition sparked mainstream popularity for Native American art and inspired a related appreciation of indigenous religious beliefs.

On the last day of the San Francisco Exposition—it lasted seven months—there was a luncheon for members of the staff who had worked in the federal building, several hundred probably, many of whom I had never met. I think one event that I recall was that Edgar Bergen and Charlie McCarthy were there. We had a young Navajo silversmith who had his wife and a child with him, and Edgar Bergen picked up the Little Navajo baby and had it talking to the crowd. The parents were really amazed.

The Federal Indian Arts and Crafts Board Exhibition, San Francisco, 1939. Indian artists and staff posed with First Lady Eleanor Roosevelt.

Mr. and Mrs. Big Turnip, an important part of our Plains Indian group, were in their sixties and a very fine couple. Mrs. Big Turnip did very fine beadwork.

I met Eleanor Roosevelt at the Museum of Modern Art, and she wrote the foreword for the book that was prepared for that particular display and one on the meeting with the Hopi artist Fred Kabotie.

The First Lady appreciated Indian art for its aesthetic form. But these native pieces boasted symbols and colors that were far more than decorative, and stories or religious meanings were associated with each object. Indian art is an intrinsic component of Native American ceremony. Its designs embody and invoke the energy of spiritual forces. Sand paintings are not merely for display but for calling healing spirits. Symbols are integral to corresponding rituals.

Frequently, Indians depict in such artwork the image of Father Sun. Tribespeople throughout the Americas incorporate sun designs into their ceremonies—only one of which is the famous sun dance. When Gladys Tantaquidgeon witnessed that dance, she was mindful that federal authorities had prohibited it in the early twentieth century. She remembered that the Mohegan Wigwam ceremony had also nearly perished due to non-Indian disapproval until Emma Baker revised and revived it. Gladys understood how that restored Wigwam held her tribe together after the Mohegan Reservation, its lands allotted in 1790, was broken up between 1861 and 1872. The tribe's request for that change had been prompted by a desire to be free of corrupt reservation overseers who sold tribal agricultural fields and burial grounds. The end of the reservation era left Mohegan Church as the only communally owned tribal property. Held outside the church, the Wigwam came to represent the endurance and solidarity of the Mohegan Tribe. With all that in mind, Gladys advocated the removal of any remaining limitations on the sun dance during her tenure on the Indian Arts and Crafts Board. In acknowledgment of that work, the Crow elder Chewing Black Bones gave Gladys his sun dance whistle to add to her Tantaquidgeon Museum treasures.

I was visiting the Crow agency, north of Billings, Montana, and the first fair I attended there was referred to as the sun dance. They build a lodge. It is circular with these big poles and branches over the top. The ceremony was "brought in" by an elderly woman, and these two younger women were escorting her from the tepee not far from the lodge. . . . At that time, the men (the dancers) were not practicing that custom of using pointed sticks like a pencil to pierce through their skin on their chest. . . . But I understand now that they have returned to that custom.

There was food passed around at certain times. My coworker Nellie Star Boy Buffalo Chief and I at the fairgrounds were not far from the museum where we worked. We were told that the attendants were like deacons in the church. Nellie explained to me that you do not thank them for the food because that was coming from the Creator. I felt a little concerned about accepting food because we were on salary, and here were some destitute families, but Nellie said, "accept the food," since she knew a family with several children and she would pass the food on.

Gladys witnessed the extraordinary power of native dances while she was out West. Eighteenth-century pressure from Christian missionaries had forced Mohegan women to stop doing most old-style dances by the nineteenth century. In the twentieth century, Mohegan men performed one war dance while singing the old song "Polly in the Hut." The western rain dance was a stereotype in popular culture. Now Gladys witnessed its truly amazing snake medicine, which straddled life and death and caused rain to dance upon scaly, dry lands.

During the summer that I attended Summer Institute in-service training school in Santa Fe, one of our friends who was well known, Fred Kabotie, he invited several of us to attend a rain dance in his village of Second Mesa. We were not far from Winslow, Arizona. We were advised to get there early and be among the first of the cars to leave. So we sat up in the high adobe house, and the dance took place in the center on the clay floor. There were four or five long poles set up in a tepee fashion and a few branches so you couldn't see the medicine man. There were the keepers of the snakes. They would pass by the tepee and reach in and hand out a snake. The dancers, each one had a younger man who would stand behind the dancer because the dancer holds a snake in his mouth. The purpose of the person behind him: if the snake's head moves around, the attendant would use the stick to tap it, so he wouldn't get close enough to bite the dancer. Then the clouds we noticed started to thicken—seems it went on most of the afternoon. Then four young men were supposed to go out to throw the snakes to the four directions. About the time they would have put the snakes down, it started to rain, and I've never seen it rain harder in my life.

Native people trusted Gladys as an envoy of the Indian Arts and Crafts Board more than they had when she was an agent of the Bureau of Indian Affairs. Her new job afforded her invitations to tribal social gatherings and private ceremonials. One feast celebrated the successful healing powers of a medicine man. That event reaffirmed her belief that when balance is restored the old medicine taught by her grandmothers could prevail. Gladys had learned to give thanks for all blessings from her great-aunt Fidelia Fielding. Fidelia had kept a daily diary of her personal thanksgivings to the Great Spirit and repeated an ongoing affirmation of thanks with the words "Mundo Wigo" (the Creator is good). Thus Gladys was well prepared to join in thanksgiving with an Indian family in Browning, Montana, not far from the Museum of the Northern Plains:

Their family lived in a log house, and this was an evening affair. It was explained to me that someone in the family had been treated by the medicine man and had been cured. This ceremony was held in recognition of the medicine man and the cure that had been effected. It was a long room, and several men were seated at the end of the room, and in the center was a kettle with some sort of soup and families around the side. Women on one side and men on the other. The speeches and songs went on for quite some time, and I was told that at midnight there would be a break in the ceremonies, and if I wished to leave, Flora Go Forth and Nellie and I could leave at that time. Before midnight break, the soup was passed around by attendants. Someone said it was buffalo tongue.

Above all else, Gladys's elders had taught her to be thankful to Mother Earth. She had learned to love every inch of the rocks, trees, and soil of Mohegan Hill and to remember the Little People who worked to protect that place. She understood that Indians, and all people, suffer bad medicine when anything destroys or contaminates the natural resources of Mother Earth.

On Mohegan Hill, Gladys had been taught that conservation and respect for Mother Earth was the only acceptable way of living. Her nanus had instructed her never to throw anything away. Stripped turkey wishbones and barren corncobs became the body-bases of dolls. Hill folk wasted nothing. She had also witnessed that same respect throughout western Indian country.

Conservation was a new national buzzword in the 1930s, and Gladys took the occasion of celebrating the birthday of the Campfire Girls organization on national radio to promote conservation of natural resources. Her aim was to kindle concern for the natural world and to heighten awareness of the indigenous values with which it is synonymous. Her typed press release for the occasion ended with a story about the greatest threat to conservation.

As a representative of my people, I wish to extend to you, the Camp Fire Girls of America, sincere congratulations on the splendid program which has been launched by your organization for the year 1938. The Conservation of Natural Resources is of vital importance to the American people.

The Indian is inherently a worshiper of nature and holds in reverence the gifts of the Creator, which are his heritage. Long ago, we are told, the Creator gave to the Indian many things: thickly wooded forests where lived game animals and where birds nested in the trees unmolested. Rivers and lakes that abounded with fish. Wild fruits, berries, and nuts were plentiful. Great herds of buffalo roamed the plains. The Indian carefully guarded those precious gifts, and wastefulness was unknown. The Indian took only what he needed for food, shelter[,] and clothing. The animals and plants, the Indian believed, had souls the same as mankind, and it was the custom of my people to recognize the spirits of the animals and plants in their prayers of Thanksgiving to the Creator. The Indian believed that so long as he obeyed the laws of Nature, there would always be an abundance of the gifts of the Creator for his use. For many, many years, the Indian practiced conservation and lived well.

Then there came a time when the scene changed. One day we are told, an old chief, looking out across the Great Water, toward the sunrise, saw a "Great White Bird" coming toward him. Its great white wings were outspread, and he seemed to be sailing on the surface of the water. The old chief hurried back to the village to tell his people. They hurried to the shore to see the "Great White Bird." As it came nearer they could see the figures of strange-looking men on its beak and wings. The chief was fearful for his people. He sadly told them that many changes would take place after the coming of the White man in his strange canoe.

So it was that the strangers came to our land of plenty.[28]

PART IV

TRAIL HOME TO THE HILL

CHAPTER 18

NANU GLADYS

Them that knows nothing fears nothing.

—GLADYS TANTAQUIDGEON

Traditional Mohegans often become ill when away from their land for too long. They miss the ancient rock places and protective good spirits of Mohegan Hill. Gladys gave up her own battle with nagging poor health and returned home in 1947. She had left Mohegan Hill in 1919 and had only visited since then. Yet during the years away, her spirit had longed to be home. Her inability to maintain good health while away from the hill reflects the extraordinarily close link between Mohegan medicine people and the land of Mohegan.

Many old-time Mohegans never leave the hill once they reach a substantial age. After Gladys came home, she strayed less and less in the decades that followed. More than half a century later, she remains steadfast in her place of balance and good medicine. She has never forgotten the tenuous nature of her health when she lived out West.

During this time in the West my health was always up and down. It seemed to be I suppose a nervous condition of the stomach, and I'm not a meat eater. So I was in and out of treatments when I was in Indian Service. The food situation was very difficult for me. I thought when I got to the western country at least there would be corn. But it was so hard and dry.

I had always had a number of ailments, had to be careful about food, had colds. . . . Mother was anxious for any members of the family that had opportunities to go away, to pursue any line of work. Of course, along the way, there was always that influence. The saddest time in my life was when I couldn't be with my family when my mother died—I was in the hospital at that time. That was a very sad time for me. Still, it was good to be back home. I think that my thoughts were always more or less there. There is something about home, that even though I might have been far away, there was always that influence from my early childhood. But in coming back home perhaps I'd never been away.

Upon her return, Gladys became a sort of celebrity among her people. No one else had gone to college, traveled the country, and enjoyed the company of celebrities like Gutzon Borglum—the man who carved Mount Rushmore. *Mademoiselle* magazine featured her in the October 1947 issue on modern Indian women; a photo caption read, "Anthropologist Gladys Tantaquidgeon, a Mohegan, makes a study of Indian designs in her Connecticut home." The glamour notwithstanding, the tone of the article was patronizing. It reminded Gladys that the next challenge of her life would be to teach the non-Indian world about Indian culture.

> To a good many Americans, Indians are a people so remote that they seem to belong to another time and place . . . [unlike popular stereotypes of them as] beings of incredible cruelty who indulge in what are generally described as nameless orgies . . . many Indians are capable and intelligent members of their communities.[29]

Having walked places few Mohegans ever dreamed about, Gladys welcomed a chance to settle into a life of nanuhood. She stopped driving a car and focused on research, writing, beading, and finger weaving as her new daily routine. She stayed fit by caring for nieces and nephews whom she challenged to games of jump rope or hide-and-seek.

Visitors who wanted an audience with Gladys either met with her at the museum or sat in her kitchen beside her woodstove. She always found time to listen over a cup of tea and crackers about a new job, having a baby, or electing a new chief.

From 1947 to 1949, she also cared for her ailing father until his passing. During his last difficult year, she remembered that artistic handiwork was healing in dark times. Out of sadness, she wrought beauty, braiding two rugs from sewing scraps. Those magnificent floor coverings grace her living room to this day.

That same year, as Gladys turned fifty, her beloved aunt Nettie Fowler, who had selected her to carry on the Church Ladies Sewing Society, passed into the spirit world. As Nanu Fowler followed the Path of the Sun onto the Beautiful White Path, Gladys knew that the last of her elder role models had left the Trail of Life. Suddenly she was fully a grandmother. Like her nanus before her, she was the one responsible for ensuring that the proper ceremonies were done at funerals. Her people called upon her, along with other tribal elders, to decide whether someone would sing the Mohegan death chant or where a burial would be at Shantok. The old generation had passed their torch.

When I returned, many of our old people were sick or had already gone, and father was in poor health. Our sister Ruth had taken care of the family—not only parents but grandmothers, aunts, different ones. She had been the mainstay and had given up opportunities to further her education. There was the time when one of my brothers was ill, and she always took care of the family.

After her father's passing, Gladys took a job at the state women's prison in Niantic. Her sisters, Ruth and Winifred, had already dedicated their careers to that institution. Ruth was the industrial supervisor of the women's sewing area, and Winnie was the executive secretary to the warden. Western Indian reservations had taught Gladys about the struggles of people with little hope, and she was optimistic that she could offer the inmates understanding. From this point onward, Gladys broadened her good medicine beyond Indian country and shared it with those in need in the larger world.

After father's death, a friend asked if I would be interested in working at what was then known as the State Farm for Women Correctional Center. So I went for an interview and visited the various buildings, different departments. I thought that, perhaps, if the superintendent saw fit to employ me, I would like to try the work there in that particular field with the women of various ages. After the interview, they told me that they would be very pleased to have me as one of the staff.

I worked in the library. There was a woman in charge, and along with the library work we had classes for some of the women. I had courses in craft-work, embroidery, crochet, knitting, and sometimes as many as twenty or twenty-five in the class. It was customary, if the matron would be off for the day, that those of us . . . assigned to the prison building worked more frequently than any of the others. That was a large brick building probably thirty to thirty-five women at the time—all the way from one woman who must have been eighty years of age (and had been at the original old prison and transferred to the Niantic facility) and to a few in their late teens. There was one I didn't feel was there for a very serious crime—I think it was neglect of children. There were those who had murdered a husband, fiancé. A few were on alcohol, and not as many on drugs at that time. And all these women were housed in the second floor of this large brick building.

The women were dressed in the same colored print dress, light grayish as I recall, and they had to wear brown oxfords and cotton stockings. On Sundays: white dresses, white shoes and stockings. Some worked in laundry some in the sewing room. A number of women worked in the barns and milked the cows and had their own milk and butter—that didn't last very long, I understand. Some worked in the kitchens. Others had cleaning assignments. There were a few who went out to the homes of staff members to work as housekeepers.

There were perhaps more rules and regulations than in Indian Service. For instance, much more to do with locks and keys than I had experienced before.

Harold Tantaquidgeon building the longhouse at Tantaquidgeon Museum during the winter of 1931–32. He is holding snowshoes from Naskapi .

For the most part, in the prison building, they visited back and forth in a friendly manner. There would be an occasional outburst. At the library, we always had a busy time. There were chorus groups. Women could come in and play piano and sing if they wanted to. Perhaps, after being on an Indian reservation, I had a little better understanding about their problems and what caused them.

During the mid-1950s, except for her work in Niantic, Gladys concentrated on "holding the fort," protecting tradition and guarding Mohegan. She joined her cousins Courtland Fowler and Loretta Fielding Schultz and her brother, Harold, in galvanizing the tribal community to repair Mohegan Church. She also became more active in Mohegan tribal government. When the church reopened in 1956 after several years of work, tribal members celebrated with an old-time Wigwam. But the postwar Red Scare had stimulated xenophobic paranoia. Many tribespeople did not attend, refusing to call attention to themselves.

Gladys countered that atmosphere of despair with her good medicine. In 1957, she optimistically added another room to Tantaquidgeon Museum to house the collection she had amassed out West. By the early 1960s, the museum averaged more than ten thousand visitors annually. Further donations of artifacts made it necessary to add a third room to the museum in 1964. Gladys was far from giving up on the Mohegans.

The museum was the place where Grandmother Gladys was training the next generation to think positively about the future. She aggressively passed on traditions even though the state of tribal affairs was discouraging.

Mohegan descendants in our family learn at an early age about their forebears. For example, Heather Montgomery, at about age four, would be at the bus stop with her great-uncle Chief Tantaquidgeon to greet the children, and after the short talk by her uncle, she would lead the way up the trail to the museum—sometimes with him or with one of the young visitors as her partner.

Last fall when a group of nursery school children came from Norwich, two Mohegans were in the group—Chip Terni and Becky Cloutier. They had the honor of leading the way up the trail. Becky's brother, Mark, now in a second grade class at our nearby Mohegan School, walked up the wooded path when the two classes visited the museum. Another Mohegan School kindergarten class set out four pine trees at the museum, and our niece Bethany Fawcett was in that group.[30]

Gladys continued her research and teaching throughout this period, and occasionally she still reached out to academia. In 1963, she conducted a lecture series at Wilson College in Pennsylvania along with the archaeologist Jeanette MacCurdy. When she went out on such rare excursions, she kept her diet simple, usually ordering grilled cheese sandwiches and amber tea. Her stomach did not do well when she was away from the hill. During the museum off-season, Gladys compiled her old notes on the medicine of the Mohegan, Delaware, and other related tribes. In 1972, at age seventy-three, she published those findings in a popular monograph titled *Folk Medicine of the Delaware and Related Algonkian Indians.*[31] She based that text on lessons learned from Medicine Man Witaponoxwe, the teachings of her Mohegan grandmothers, and the traditions of other eastern tribes like the Cayuga and Nanticoke.

Gladys's leisure time in the 1970s and 1980s included regular five o'clock telephone conversations with her niece Hatti, the eldest child of her late sister Lillian. Hatti was a round little woman who made magic with her big chuckling laugh. She was the tribal fortune-teller, a marvelous seamstress, and the keeper of secret family recipes. Gladys needed the jovial afternoon exchanges with Hatti to counter the fact that Mohegan Hill had become a politically volatile place. Varying attitudes toward tribal land claim suits divided the Mohegans. Still, Gladys focused on solving these disputes by staying close to the Creator and following the example of her nanus. Like Emma Baker, she maintained the tribal rolls and corresponded with hundreds of tribal members. She also worked on creating a written tribal constitution in 1970. That year, she was elected vice-chair of the Tribal Council and recommended that the new chair, Courtland Fowler, become the next Mohegan chief. After a meeting, the elders informally named Courtland Chief Little Hatchet. During the 1970s, neither the sovereign authority of chiefs (outlawed by Connecticut in 1769) nor the spiritual title of medicine women (ridiculed from the eighteenth through most of the twentieth century) was widely broadcast by Mohegans, as a result of continued mainstream denigration of native rights and religious beliefs.

Some two decades later, in 1992, the Mohegans formally conveyed Courtland's posthumous title. The tribe also bestowed an official medicine title upon Gladys and (posthumously) on Emma Baker. These installations took place in August at the annual Wigwam festival. The tribe also named

Ralph Sturges its new chief. As Gladys placed the ceremonial roach on his head, she gave him the name G'tinemong, meaning He who helps thee.

Gladys did not like her new title. She said she never felt worthy of it, which is precisely why she was perfect for the job. The formal restoration of that ancient title gave confidence to the tribal community and prompted a flood of good spirits.

That year also marked the anniversary of America's first ethnic-cleansing program initiated by Christopher Columbus. Consequently, many good-spirited non-Indians acknowledged the need to begin a healing time. That five-hundred-year legacy of infamy inspired a national group called Church Women United to disavow the desecration of Indian religious beliefs by early missionaries. The local organizational branch requested a gathering at Mohegan Church. Gladys attended the event and nodded as the Delaware-Mohegan creation story echoed from the Mohegan Church pulpit for the first time. Indians on the hill saw that the circle begun five hundred years before was turning 'round.

CHAPTER 19

TALKING ARTIFACTS

Observe, concentrate and remember.

—GLADYS and HAROLD TANTAQUIDGEON

In 1995, another story relating to Mohegan Church unfolded. During a re-patriation research trip, members of the tribe's Cultural Resources Department discovered an elm bark box at the Peabody and Essex Museum in Salem, Massachusetts. When they showed a photo of it to Gladys, her response was that it "looks like the one from Oneida." In the eighteenth and early nineteenth centuries, Oneida was the place to which many church-going Mohegans had relocated.

After hearing Gladys's brief recollection, one of the tribal members who handled the box had dreams about it. Gladys explained that such dreams were the best way to uncover information about things. Through these dreams, the tribe discovered that migrating Mohegans had sent this heavily inscribed box home several centuries ago as a record of their journey. Like most native artifacts, this one had been appropriated first by an anthropologist and then by a non-Indian museum. Originally, the Mohegan minister Samson Occum, had dispatched the box from Oneida to his sister, Lucy Occum (the founder of Mohegan Church). Its inscriptions were of ancient form and included a complex version of the Trail of Life—Path of the Sun—Beautiful White Path design. Upon receiving the tribe's documentation, the Peabody and Essex Museum returned the elm bark box to the Mohegans. With encouragement from Gladys, tribal members used dream-messages to decipher its meaning:

In the late eighteenth century, the Mohegan people set out westward following the path of the setting sun.

From six different other local tribes (seven tribes including the Mohegans), varying numbers of families left in assorted groupings. The Mohegans, the Eastern Pequots, and the Western Pequots come from the same root. Some tribal people stayed close to their tribal homelands, while others left. In every tribe there is a circular link between past, present, and future. The Mohegan, Eastern Pequots, Western Pequots, Narragansetts, Montauks, Nehantics, Tunxis eventually reached Oneida territory. Some continued west from New York to Wisconsin. The seven tribes joined there as one in a circle of unity.

Gladys helped interpret other missing artifacts. A "talkative" mask was found on a similar repatriation visit that year to the University of Pennsylvania, where she had studied and worked. Emma Baker had taught Gladys about the use of masks in ancient healing ceremonies, and Witaponoxwe had given her one of these masks. Gladys's brother Harold had also made two. On seeing a picture of a crooked-nose mask housed there, Gladys recognized it as one of those made by her brother. She recalled his wearing it during the annual Wigwam for the general casting out of bad spirits. The tribal pipe carrier Ernest Gilman and Dorothy Long and Red Moon (Laurence Schultz) of the Council of Elders shared that recollection. Gladys explained that Mohegans carved such masks from living trees, to enliven them. These masks also cohosted the spirit of their maker and evoked the powerful aide of Gunci Mundo, the Great Spirit.

When the tribe requested that the crooked-nose mask be returned permanently as a sacred object under federal repatriation law, the University of Pennsylvania refused; the grounds for denying the request included the fact that Frank Speck had not recorded the connection of masks to Mohegan religion. Once again, Speck had failed to appreciate indigenous beliefs fully. As a result, the tribe suffered the effects of white academia's limited comprehension. When Gladys considered objects created by native peoples, she not only understood and respected their value, she also ackowledged that each of them offered lessons for her own life trail.

Chief Matahga and Harold Tantaquidgeon, circa 1930. Matahga holds a crooked-nose mask.

A walk through the Tantaquidgeon Museum is a consolidated walk along Gladys's life trail. She calls the entry room home because it contains Algonquian and East Coast artifacts. The room's ceiling centerpiece is the Penobscot birch bark canoe that Gladys received while visiting that tribe to conduct an educational survey. Close by are snowshoes, dog moccasins, and partleche (painted animal skin) clothing given to her as kinship gifts during her Montagnais Naskapi trip. Baskets for Granny Squannit, leader of the Little People, made by the Wampanoags sit in cases across the way. They acknowledge shared appreciation of those religious beliefs. Nearby is a turtle shell cup and rattle from her Delaware colleague, Medicine Man Witaponoxwe. Beaded handbags and pincushions sewn by her three nanus hang proudly in a case beside similar pieces by modern tribal members.

Around the corner, painted wood splint baskets, carved spoons, scoops, and puddin' sticks made by her father, John, her brother Harold, her cousin Roscoe Skeesucks, and her uncle Chief Matahga cover rows of shelving. Hung on the ceiling just above them is the rocking chair that belonged to Martha Uncas, grandmother and mentor of Fidelia Fielding, who taught Gladys about the Little People. Gladys's regalia holds the place of honor in the front room. It includes her spirit belt (given in recognition of her responsibility to the Little People) and a collar and skirt beaded with the Trail of Life.

The back room of the museum is a stroll into another chapter in Gladys's life. Exhibited here are the life-styles and art ways of the Indian people of the West, where she served as a community worker and native arts promoter. The brilliant colors of the West emerge in bold contrast to the deep woodland hues of the other rooms. Gladys devoted the lefthand section to the Sioux, among whom she found friends who accepted her as a granddaughter. In 1940, her coworker, Nellie Star Boy Buffalo Chief, gave her a pipe bag from Rosebud, which hangs above a basket given to her by her neighbor Mrs. Afraid of Hawk. Two unhappy short-haired dolls presented to her by the Yankton Sioux stand next to a miniature tepee. These sad sentries are reminiscent of the tragedies Gladys witnessed while working among those people. Hanging above them is the sun dance whistle of Chewing Black Bones, reminding her of the restoration of that ceremony. Nearby a pair of Crow moccasins and leggings also recalls Billings, Montana, in 1939.

The museum's exhibits represent lessons in Gladys's life. When she tells about the pieces, she likes to tap a talking stick to help the stories stay in the listeners' memory. Those lessons along her medicine trail give the Mohegan people a link to their own earlier traditions and the rest of Native America as well.

Like Gladys's, Harold Tantaquidgeon's life trail meanders through the artifacts at Tantaquidgeon Museum. Harold built the structure in 1931, along with their father, John. He made his mark on the original building by carving a blue stone medicine diamond and placing it into the chimney. When he built the museum's first room, he placed local arrowheads into the mortar by the woodstove's pipe to bless it.

He constructed a longhouse and wigwam behind the museum where he taught valuable outdoor survival skills to local Mohegans, scout troops, and 4-H members. Harold believed that survival training was a practical necessity. As a fighter squadron tail gunner during World War II, he was shot down in the New Guinea jungles; only his native skills enabled him and the other three crewmembers to survive the long weeks until rescue. Harold determined edible foodstuffs and carved tools with which to build a shelter. Back home on the hill, his military medals appear at the museum alongside his Indian clothes, all part of his regalia. Harold also displayed his war helmets beside his feather headdresses, stating that all those hats were headdresses of an Indian chief who fought for the land he loved.

That museum, a tiny stone structure covered with ivy, was the center of Harold's universe. His younger sister, Ruth, recalls him grabbing a hose from a tottering fireman when their family home burst into flames from a chimney fire in 1935. He raced to spray the trees between the house and the museum, knowing that the house was replaceable but the treasures in the museum were not.

Harold devoted all his years following the Korean War to making the traditional things of the past, just as his father had done until his passing in 1949. He filled the museum's cases with carved wooden cups, baskets, scoops, bowls, spoons, hearth brooms, crossbows, stone pipes, hatchets, arm guards, quivers, crooked knives, awls, dippers, drums, and bows. Those were the things of stone, bone, and wood that made up the traditional Mohegan world. Born in 1904, Harold was slowing down by the 1980s. He gave up even his regular once-a-year trip to pick up a Thanksgiving turkey, with his niece Catherine Lamphere. Like Gladys, Chief Uncas, and many other traditional Mohegans before him, Chief Harold Tantaquidgeon chose to spend his last days upon the Trail of Life atop Mohegan Hill, passing into the spirit world in April of 1989.

September 20, 1978. Mohegan School Grade two visits the museum:

One might call this "October's Bright Blue Weather." A bright clear morning and as we listen closely the sound of voices tells us that our three second grade classes are approaching the trail leading to the museum. This group of pupils, teachers, and parents (57 children, seven adults) are from Mohegan School about ¾ mile northeast of the museum. Chief Tantaquidgeon meets the group where Mohegan Church Lane joins the museum trail and chooses two members to lead the way to the area where they will be seated. It is a wonderful sight to see these children take their places on the benches and wait for Chief to give them a little Mohegan background. When greeted, he asked "Do I know anyone here?" A small blonde boy said, "Hi Tom" [short for the nickname Tomahawk]. This from Mark Cloutier II, great great grandson of our older sister Lillian Tantaquidgeon Strickland.

Wearing a cowboy ha[t] and a patch bearing his mark, an X with four dots, Chief sets the group of benches in the shade of red maple, white oak, dogwood, mountain ash and catalpa ... We try to prepare the teachers and students in advance so they will not expect to see us in ceremonial Indian dress. Our type of wigwam and long house dwelling are new to many. All are soon at ease and Chief Tantaquidgeon tells them about Chief Uncas of long ago who lived nearby and walked where they are sitting. . . . There's fun and laughter and the children learn firsthand about Mohegan Indian life past and present. After comes a story about the Reverend Samson Occum. . . . It is time for the group to join Chief at the table and select an item about which he or she may want to inquire. It may be the small drum or a tiny doll in a cradle board ... the story of corn is always of great interest. What it meant to Indians and Pilgrims as a means of survival in early days. . . . Next the group visits the long house bordered by our sacred red cedars. This is an exciting moment for most children once they enter through the low opening in the east end ... and wait on low benches on either side, many are transported back hundreds of years in their imagination. Chief is seated on a low frame bed covered with buffalo hide. Traditionally it was customary for males and females to sit on opposite sides. A fireplace in the center is framed by a circle of stones. Clothing, cooking utensils, a mortar and pestle for grinding corn, baskets and a bow and arrow are some of the things in view. The frame of the long house is made of hickory saplings that Chief placed in the ground and bent to form arches when lashed together with narrow strips of hickory bark. Canvas covers the frame in place of the traditional bark or mats made from cattail flag or corn husk. Outside the group will stop to hear Chief explain and demonstrate how the stone mortars and bowls were made. He will then select several children to take a smooth round stone and turn it around in another stone hollowed out by the many children and adults who have part-icipated in this ritual. Next the group, peeks into the smaller wigwam then moves on to the shed used for shelter for classes on rainy days. Benches are like bleachers and a long table displays woodworking tools, in sight as well are clubs carved like different woodland animals.[32]

Harold's cultivation of good relations with non-Indian visitors to the museum cleared a smooth trail for those Mohegans who followed him. Of the children who came, he would often say, "Who knows, one day when some of them grow up to become congressmen and senators voting on In-dian issues, maybe their visit here will guide them to vote the right way."

CHAPTER 20

RESTORING THE
MOHEGAN NATION

The dying days are done. The cycle of life has begun anew.
—JAYNE FAWCETT at the Mohegan Reservation ground blessing,
November 1995

Gladys learned early in life that the Mohegans' relationship with non-Indians began with treaties between Mohegan sachems and English kings.
Her nanus taught her that after the American Revolution Mohegan leaders
signed accords with the Connecticut leaders but remained wary of the
United States government. Bad federal policies and laws like the Indian
Removal Act of 1830 encouraged Mohegans to avoid a federal relationship
for some time. However, by the 1970s, services to American Indians were
predicated on such relationships. Thus, in 1978, the tribe began the process of applying for federal recognition as a sovereign Indian nation.

Gladys worked for recognition until 1984 when she resigned as vice-chair
of the Mohegan Tribe. Although eighty-five that year, she did not fully retire from tribal involvement. For the next decade, she and her sister Ruth
devoted themselves to the tribe's research effort by organizing documents
in their home. After reviewing twenty thousand pages of paper work, the
federal government formally recognized the Mohegan people on March 7,
1994. That day, the assistant secretary of the interior Ada E. Deer (a
Menominee) phoned the Mohegan tribal office, which was across the street
from Gladys's home, to inform Chief G'tinemong. Upon hearing the news,
everyone present jumped, cheered, and cried. One tribal councilor sobbed,

"After all these years, all these years." Another said, "Welcome to Mohegan—that's what Harold Tantaquidgeon used to say. But really, welcome to the Mohegan Nation for the first time."

In response to the news Gladys replied calmly, "That's wonderful. Now what do we do next?" Gladys was right in asking that sobering question. She understood better than anyone that even such a grand moment is no more than a small step along the life trail of a people. She then cautioned them with the advice of a young Yankton Sioux she had met in the 1930s:

Remember to take the best of what the white man has to offer . . . and use it to still be Indian.

Gladys's work of educating the world about the Mohegans facilitated miraculous changes for her tribe. On September 30, 1995, the Mohegans purchased 240 acres of what had been their northernmost reservation lands and placed them in federal trust. The new Mohegan Reservation was in the same place as the one disbanded during Emma Baker's day. There, on the Thames River's western banks, the Mohegan Nation reclaimed its home. Gladys had kept her people focused on what was important.

On May 15, 1998, on the four-hundredth birthday of Sachem Uncas, the tribe bought back his ancient village of Shantok, which had been taken by the state of Connecticut for parklands in 1926. When that deal was completed, Gladys responded "'bout time!" Again, the Mohegans remembered to give thanks as Gladys had taught them. Her great-nephew Pipe Carrier Ernest Gilman and great-grandnephew Fire Keeper Tom Epps lit thirteen fires to commemorate the occasion. Thirteen signifies one complete circle, since there are thirteen moons in an Indian year, thirteen sections on the back of the patient turtle, and thirteen generations since Uncas.

Nanu Gladys had taught her children well. On each of these special occasions, they remembered their ancestors with ceremony, just as Gladys's nanus had taught her to do. At the reservation's 1995 ground blessing, the vice-chair of the Tribal Council, Gladys's niece, my mother, Jayne Fawcett, summed up the lifeways and life trail of the Mohegan people that Gladys had for so long sustained:

Aquai koh weegun tah. Greetings and Good Day.

November is here. The nights are longer. It is the time for storytelling. This is a story about survival, our survival, the survival of the Mohegan spirit, and it begins the way our stories have always begun, with the words "Listen and never forget it."

Thirteen generations have passed since our grandfather Uncas brought us to this cove and to these hills. He was a man of might and power, and his domain encompassed much of what is now Connecticut. Yet he lived in a fearful time. Others more powerful than he had invaded his territory. The woods of Mohegan no longer belonged to his people alone. Somehow he had to find a way for his people to survive.

He found his answer in the ancient "lesson of the broken arrow," symbol of peace and friendship. Uncas pledged his friendship to the newcomers with the formal offering of his heart saying, "This heart is

Gladys with students at Tantaquidgeon Museum, circa 1975.

not mine it is yours." The Mohegan pattern of survival through friend-ship had begun.

"Survival has always been number one with our people." Those words were written by my oldest daughter in a college history paper. In the margins, her professor scribbled in red ink, "What good is mere survival?"

"Mere survival?"

Think about it. Without it there would have been nothing else. There would have been no better day . . . and no today. A unique part of mankind would have been lost forever.

Every Mohegan here today is a living testimonial to the wisdom of Uncas'[s] strategy of survival through friendship. We are all descendants of that great man. He continues to be the force that binds us together in the bonds of family and tradition.

We have sustained each other through the dying days—those dying days when we were told that Ben Uncas [sachem 1726–69] would be the last Chief; Fidelia Fielding the last speaker of our language; Emma Baker the last medicine woman; John Tantaquidgeon, the last basketmaker; nanu Fowler's Wigwam, the last Green Corn Festival; and Mary Storey's vision of pale strangers swallowing us up forever a reality.

Each of the five families, Storey, Fowler, Fielding, Baker and Tantaquidgeon has played an integral part in the survival process. Each family has fulfilled the wishes of grandfather Uncas throughout the thirteen generations since his passing.

Like the thirteen sections on the back of the turtle marking the thirteen moons or months of our year, or one full cycle, those of the thirteeth generation from Uncas have come full cycle.

We have heard our final "last." The "dying days" are done. The cycle of life has begun anew. Uncas['s] way of survival has prevailed.

Now we move forward to a new way beyond survival that will bring the restoration of our language and traditions together with the spirit sounds of the Makiawisug, the little people who inhabit these lands beside this river.

Here at this Trading Cove the Mohegans will once again conduct their business.

With the help of our dedicated backers and our good friends and neighbors, we can say once again with pride, "Welcome to Mohegan, Land of Uncas, Homeland of the Mohegan People."

Mundu Wigo—"The Creator is Good." Tawbut nee, "Thank You."[33]

After the 1996 creation of the Mohegan Sun Casino on the tribe's reservation site, the tribe carried out many good-spirited works begun by Gladys. Today the Mohegans operate a Lakota Sioux aid program, the Little People Company (to create cultural education products and certify and promote authentic Native American arts), the Corn Project (to cultivate the ancient eight-row flint corn used to make yokeag at the old Wigwams), the Mohegan Language Restoration Project, the Shantok Restoration Project, the Mohegan Church Restoration Project, and the Uncas Memorial Project (at the site of the massive Norwich desecration observed by Emma Baker). Tribal government is converting Fort Hill into an elderly housing center and restoring headstones at burial grounds. Gladys's life's work provided the Mohegans with clear direction. Her lessons made these things happen— with a little help from the good spirits of Mohegan Hill.

PART V

TRAIL TO MEDICINE

CHAPTER 21

A DAY WITH GLADYS
AT NINETY-EIGHT

In my earlier years, I perhaps wasn't aware of the fact that time was going by so rapidly ... and later I realized that ... many of our old people were dying and their knowledge went with them. Something had to be done to preserve a record of their way of life. It was a little bit difficult because I couldn't devote the entire time to this type of project and it was just hit or miss. My goal has always been that this information ... be passed on to future generations.

—GLADYS TANTAQUIDGEON

The day when Gladys and Ruth serve the first succotash every year draws great-grandnieces and -nephews to their house. Mohegan children wave homemade flags and sing to honor the first of the corn and bean harvest. "It's succotash time, It's succotash time, It's succotash time again!" goes the song that begins one of Gladys's favorite days. May 1 is yet another of her cherished annual holidays. That is the day when Tantaquidgeon Museum opens every year. Gladys's favorite times are always those days that honor tradition atop Mohegan Hill.

A typical May first varies little. Gladys maintains a set routine awakening with the birds—mourning doves, robins, cardinals, and blue jays interspersed with dozens of crows and the occasional hawk and eagle passerby. Before dawn, she has a good breakfast of a small cup of tan coffee, toast, and cereal with banana and wheat germ. She likes to eat in the oakey kitchen beside her white cast-iron woodstove. Her standard attire is a simple paisley dress with one of her own finger-woven belts and a silver-and-turquoise Navajo brooch.

When nine o'clock rolls around, she makes her way up the hill to the museum. As the day goes on, she takes a break from her work to come down to the house and sip a cup of amber tea with sugar and nibble a few crackers. Between visitors, she might snack on two or three chips. At noontime, if she can break away long enough, she loves to fix herself a Velveeta and marmalade sandwich or some creamed chipped beef and hard-boiled egg on toast. If a niece or nephew stops by with a cold, she will laughingly prescribe "some boneset tea, cold in the daytime and hot at night." If her visitor is feverish, she will recommend some mint. She might also suggest an offering to the Little People to make life go smoothly.

During any given day, Gladys is host to many visitors, both friends and strangers. Some stay for hours, hoping to learn in a morning or an afternoon the truths they have been seeking a lifetime. Sometimes they find them.

Editor:

A few years ago when my husband's seven- year-old grandson visited us from Texas, we were at a loss as to what to do after weeks of monsoon rains. Having heard of a Tantaquidgeon Museum, I called. A woman said it was closed but to bring him down and she would open it for us.

Following her directions we were greeted by a soft-spoken, gentle little woman. I asked for the person I had spoken to and learned it was she, Gladys Tantaquidgeon, who would take us. I demurred but she insisted and, wrapping a shawl about her, she climbed the hill of rock steps by the cascading water and unlocked the little, unheated museum. She then proceeded to mesmerize this boy so far from home, encouraging him to touch and examine everything while weaving a story of the Mohegans. She refused to let us hurry him. It was a magical time in that hushed building with rain beating on the roof and a boy immersed in Indian lore.

She has no idea the effect she had on this child. To this day he asks about her. She made a deep mark on his life that dreary afternoon—and on ours. If the world had more people like Gladys Tantaquidgeon we wouldn't have to worry about our children. Hers is a gift that touched a child's life forever and left him the better for it.

I believe that each of us influences every child's life, even if [it's] just a smile as we pass by. This dear lady gave much more than was necessary. We shall be forever grateful. We thank Gladys Tantaquidgeon. Her "medicine" comes from within your soul. She is a very special memory for my husband, his grandson, and me.

Constance R. Lafleur
Danielson, [Conn.,] June 16[34]

That is what is known as Umbusk Wigo, Good Medicine.

CHAPTER 22

HAPPY HUNDREDTH BIRTHDAY

You were chosen by the Creator, which was a very good choice of a medicine woman.... I hope you live forever so you can keep continuing your journey, and we will keep giving you our respect. I hope you have a great one hundredth birthday. Thank you for giving us care.

—DAVID UNCAS SAYET, age 8, great-grandnephew of
Gladys Tantaquidgeon, June 15, 1999

The guest list included only good spirits. All others were denied entry. Volunteers draped a big white tent at Shantok, Uncas's village, in red and blue ribbons. A banner read "Happy 100th Birthday Gladys" on a simply perfect Strawberry Moon day.

In preparation for Gladys's arrival, Fire Keeper Tom Epps tended a ceremonial cedar fire, Pipe Carrier Ernest Gilman smudged the tent with sweet grass, and tribal drummers sang the welcome song. Mohegans met the obligations to their ancestors.

Gladys entered beside her sister, Ruth, shortly before noon, greeted by hundreds of well-wishers. Wearing a light blue suit, she smiled and nodded warmly to all who approached. As guests arrived, tribal hosts presented them with medallion necklaces decorated with the Trail of Life symbol framing the words "Gladys Tantaquidgeon 100th Year Celebration, 1899–1999." Greeters also offered braids of sweet grass tied with tobacco and turkey feathers as gifts.

The Council of Elders presented Gladys with a tiny gift basket, just right for offerings to the Little People. Inside was a miniature mortar and pestle, along with a small spoon, fork, and knife carved out of maple by Dan Heberding, the great-grandson of Chief Matahga (Burrill Fielding). Dan himself gave Gladys a large wooden spoon with a wolf carved on the handle.

In keeping with Indian custom, all the Native American leaders present offered Gladys the gift of words. Speaking first, for the Mohegan Tribal Council, Chairman Roland Harris offered the following commendation:

> Our [Mohegan] nation is as great as it is today because of Gladys. She's taught us how to be friends with our neighbors. She's taught us to be proud of our nation. It's a great day for Mohegan.

Chairman Kenneth Reels of the Mashantucket Pequot Tribe honored Gladys with an eagle feather and the following statement:

> Thank you for what you did for our people. Thank you for preserving the heritage of the Pequot people and keeping our ways alive. . . . The eagle climbs the highest and also represents balance, integrity and honor. We give this feather to you because that's what you represent to us.

James Cunha, the Paucatuck Pequot chief, warmly recalled his grandfather's stories about Gladys when he was a child. Representing the Narragansett Nation, Eleanor Dove declared Gladys to be "the leader of all Native Americans" and "a role model in her life." Mashpee Wampanoag tribal members from the Harding family heartily thanked Gladys for the work she did "recording so many of their tribe's ancient traditions." Contessa Big Crow, representing the Sioux Nation, conveyed deep appreciation from her tribal leaders for Gladys's "commitment to the Yankton and Pine Ridge Sioux communities in the 1930s." As representatives from each tribe spoke, the fire keeper noted that flames rose, nourished by their words.

Town, state, and federal officials also saluted Gladys, acknowledging their reciprocal relationship with her tribe. Sidney Holbrook, chief of staff for Governor John G. Rowland, read a proclamation declaring June 15, 1999, to be Gladys Tantaquidgeon Day in Connecticut. The mayor of Montville thanked Gladys for her contributions to the town, especially her work at Tantaquidgeon Museum. Congressman Sam Gejdenson, a former 4-H student of Harold Tantaquidgeon's, offered the following words in a letter:

> Yours has been a meaningful life in the fullest measure of that term, marked by achievements on many fronts, and highlighted, of course, by your work in preserving the Tribe's culture, which became the key component in maintaining its identity while moving into its current economic prominence.[35]

The Abenaki writer Joseph Bruchac presented Gladys with a song for her birthday, which all who attended the gathering sang. It concluded with the following words:

> With stubborn courage she kept the trail
> When others doubted she did not fail.
> The road of stars is still shining on
> Medicine Woman of Mohegan

After a blessing by Ernest Gilman came lunch: clam chowder, corn chowder, and turkey sandwiches. Dessert included ice cream and three birthday cakes, decorated with a turtle, a turkey, and a wolf symbolizing the three clans of the Mohegan's Lenni Lenape ancestors; a fourth cake boasted a tribal logo. Yet another carried an image of an eagle.

The tribe's newspaper, *Ni Ya Yo* (1:11), published a special edition for the event. A cover graphic featured Gladys with a smudge pot creating a trail of smoke rising up into the stars and forming an eagle, a turtle, corn, and a bear. There were articles highlighting Gladys's life's work and the following letter of thanks written by the tribal historian:

> Dear Gladys,
>
> You have dedicated your life to promoting respect for the traditions of Indian nations. You have reminded us, your Mohegan people, *never* to forget who we are. We thank you for your many gifts to the twentieth century. They have cleared our pathway to tomorrow and made better lifetrails for all who have known you. . . .

Gladys beaming at her hundredth
birthday party, held at Shantok,
Uncas's village, June 15, 1999.

Thank you for *founding Tantaquidgeon Museum* with your father,
John, and brother, Harold, in 1931. That institution is today the oldest
Indian-run museum in America.

Thank you for *providing Community Education* by inviting school
groups and individuals to visit the museum and learn about Mohegan
and other American Indian lifeways, free of charge. You have been an
inspiration to modern-day multicultural education and enriched the
lives of all who have visited your museum.

Thank you for *ensuring Friendly Relations in Our Town* by carrying
on the tradition of good associations with the non-Indian community,
first begun by Mohegan Sachem Uncas in the seventeenth century.

Thank you for *fighting for the Civil Rights* of all people. In 1934, when
you removed an Indian woman from the back of a bus in Virginia, you
took a stand on behalf of all people of color.

Thank you for *bringing Social Justice to Prison.* Your positive attitude
and work there gave inspiration to many women with little hope.

Thank you for *supporting Traditional Mohegan Religion* even when faced with serious misunderstandings of those spiritual beliefs. When you encountered the negative notion that Granny Squannit (leader of the magical Little People of the woodlands) was "a pagan woman's god" you countered that attack by unveiling her inner beauty for all to see.

Thank you for *working to Preserve the Environment* through conservation. You taught children to use things they normally would throw away, like saving wishbones and corncobs to make the body-bases for dolls. You also reminded us of many other everyday ways to care for Mother Earth.

Thank you for *facilitating the end of the Federal Indian Boarding School System*, which tore young Indians from their families, denying them the traditional training of their elders. You supported Indian people in their right to maintain their ancient systems of education.

Thank you for *fostering Indian Economic Development* through promotion of Indian Art and other sustainable enterprises.

Thank you for *passing on traditional Native herbal remedies.* By working with the grandmothers and grandfathers of Mohegan, Wampanoag, Delaware, Nanticoke and others you have been able to record this region's indigenous pharmacopeia, now recognized by the general public as a wellspring of powerful medicinal healing.

Thank you for *fighting to Save Traditional Ceremonies* like the Sundance, Raindance, and Wigwam. When you worked for the Bureau of Indian Affairs and Federal Indian Arts and Crafts Board, you countered old federal policies aimed at eradicating Indian ceremonies. At home in Mohegan, you took over as head of the Women's Sewing Society (which ran the Wigwam/Green Corn Festival) after the retirement of your aunt, nanu (Nettie) Fowler.

Thank you for *preserving the Meaning of our Ancient Symbols.* Because you passed on the meaning of these designs, your people have been able to incorporate them in contemporary buildings, publications and exhibits, enriching the lives of all who see them with the wisdom of ancient knowledge.

Thank you for *passing on our Old Stories.* Whether it is through tales of Moshup the Giant, Chahnameed the Trickster or Granny Squannit of the Little People, you have created an extraordinary storytelling legacy among your people.

Most of all, thank you for all of the intangibles of your Good Medicine. By constantly reminding the world of all that the Mohegans have been, you inspire your people to complete the circle and fulfill their destiny. You also impel others to reach genuinely within themselves, in search of their own deeper pathways to understanding.

Mundu Wigo / The Creator Is Good

Besides Gladys's contributions to her tribe, other tribes, and the non-Indian world, she has given joy and meaning to the everyday lives of her family members. Her nieces and nephews number in the hundreds, and they include many thankful men, women, and children—of whom I am one.

EPILOGUE

Gladys and Me

The teaching of Indian history to provide Indian children with a true history of their country, so they can see themselves as part of this history ... this is my wish.

—BENJAMIN BLACK ELK, Oglala Sioux

Like many Mohegans, I know Dr. Gladys Tantaquidgeon as Aunt Glady. Her late sister Harriet Winifred Tantaquidgeon Grandchamp was my grandmother. Winnie had only one child, my mother, Jayne, whom she raised in the Little House next to Gladys's home. That cozy structure was barely big enough to serve later as Winnie's garage. Some of the hill folk, like Pauline Brown, called it the honeymoon cottage, since so many Mohegans spent their early married lives there.

After Jayne grew up, she attended college and married but never left Mohegan. She and her husband, Richard Fawcett, soon moved into another tiny house on Mohegan Hill, on the old Samson Occum property. That is where I was born—on Occum Lane. Like most of the old roads in Mohegan, this one was a dirt cart path. The state and federal government had not yet settled their land claims with the Mohegans, and the town was not ready to invest in paved roads it did not really own. Even in the midsixties, Occum Lane was paved only with leftover coal cinders shoveled in 1947 by Jayne's father, Alfred, and cousin, Red Moon (Laurence Schultz).

The road's namesake, Samson Occum, was a legendary eighteenth-century Mohegan minister and teacher. He founded an Indian school that is today known as Dartmouth College. As a toddler living in the Occum house,

I considered him one of my closest friends. A window seat was my favorite sitting spot. From there, I could look outside and view all the many beings that children can see, if properly encouraged to do so. Some might say Occum, and those other beings, were my imaginary friends, but the Indians who raised me knew better.

A stone path led from my house to my grandmother Winnie's more modern dwelling next door. On weekends, I often stayed overnight there or at Gladys's home. She loved to play jump rope with me on the sidewalk leading up to the museum. Rainy days included endless card games of Old Maid, which frequently ended with my losing, as Gladys slapped her knee and exclaimed, "Oh my!" With every slap, my face grew redder.

When I was four, my parents moved to a larger home about two miles west, on Fitch Hill Road. There I had more plant and rock people to spark my imagination. That yard was wooded, with acres of huckleberries, blueberries, lady's slippers, mica, and quartz. I was particularly fond of perching on "our cliffs" (rock faces created by highway blasting) and visiting "our stream" (a tiny highway culvert). My sister, Bethany, was not born until I was seven, so the plants and rocks were among my closest early childhood friends.

Sundays, we always ate dinner with the "folks on the hill." Joining my immediate family, Gladys, Ruth, Winnie, and Harold were the Lampheres: Aunt Katy (a daughter of Gladys's late sister Lillian), Uncle Charlie (Katy's husband), Aunt Hatti (also Lillian's daughter), and Katy's girls—Dori and Bootie. I usually arrived early, walking down Church Lane to the Tantaquidgeon house right after Sunday school at Mohegan Church. My standard breakfast was leftover baked beans with wheat toast and sliced tomato. Since my grandmother had married a French Canadian, café au lait accompanied it. *That* was a cosmopolitan drink on Mohegan Hill.

When I was seven, my grandfather passed on, and my grandmother moved in with Gladys, her sister, Ruth, and brother, Harold. So my wonderful weekends with Gladys were more frequent. Each room at the Tantaquidgeon house had its own carefully selected hue. Harold's bedroom was a brave tan, accented with red-and-brown Navajo rugs. Ruth chose spirit blue and she never wore any other color. Winnie picked rose, which likewise matched her favorite perfume and lotion scent. And Gladys—you guessed it—chose sunny yellow. A sleepover at Gladys's house meant a 4:30 a.m. wake-up call with banging pots and pans rattling against the woodstove. Since I am an early riser, born to night-owl parents, I loved to stay with Gladys.

A typical twelve o'clock dinner at the Tantaquidgeons' was either "soup on the hill," stewed chicken and biscuits, "beef chuck with guck" (beef roasted with stewed tomatoes, onions, and peppers), succotash or oyster stew. For us children, Ruthy's "magic drawer" held untold treasures of puzzles, candy, and games. Ruth would also send home "blue-plate specials" with anyone who might not want to cook supper or had a family member too sick to attend. After eating, we sang songs by the piano as Ruth played by ear. My mother sang soprano, and Gladys harmonized the alto melody. When my piano playing became tolerable enough, they occasionally asked me to play, which was also my way out of doing any dinner dishes. Finally, the men went about their business. Meanwhile, Hatti took the women back to the cleared-off dining room table, to read tea leaf fortunes. As it neared time to leave, the women reconvened to discuss everyday matters and, of course, the current state of tribal affairs.

Whenever school groups, or older academic classes, visited the museum on Sundays—or any other time we were not in school—Harold and Gladys called upon Dori, Bootie, and me to serve as tour guides at Tantaquidgeon Museum. I was the youngest of our threesome but clearly the most talkative. Before and after such groups, the Sunday dinner gang would discuss "who *they* were" and "whether or not *they* seemed to learn anything during their visit." Much of the talk, in that era of the 1960s and early 1970s, focused on the "hippies" who passed through: how they dressed, whether they washed, if they supported the war in Vietnam, and if it were all right for us kids to be alone with them. Hippies were a curiosity on Mohegan Hill. They usually thought their long hair and love of nature made them acceptable to Indians, but their disrespect for tradition made the hill folk uneasy.

My visits to the Tantaquidgeon home were not limited to weekends. In 1965, I began attending Mohegan School. I took the bus there each morning, but in the afternoon I walked home to Gladys's house on the hill. My cousin, David Fowler, lived across the street from Gladys. He was the same age as I, and my great-uncle Harold told him he was to ensure that I got home safely. Harold greeted us each day with bird whistles while he chopped wood or whittled his wooden spoons. Then, he religiously sat us down for our daily quiz on what was going on in school. Harold needed to quiz those who ventured outside because he rarely left Mohegan Hill. Following the quiz, there was usually a lecture on the interconnectedness of the past, present, and future states of humankind. A favorite topic was "how the European settlers had copied our longhouses to make their covered wagons, Quonset huts, and modern RV's." Gladys or Ruth would eventually tear me away so that they, too, could quiz me. After that, David was on his own, until his grandfather, Courtland, scooped him up for further interrogation and instruction.

Once I was in the clutches of my great aunts, it was project time. I was *always* supposed to be working on something. It all began with little projects—like the making of corncob dolls out of felt scraps and pins. Then, I graduated to beaded puzzle pouches, then wishbone dolls, and ultimately finger-woven belts. *And then there was the sewing.* Everyone on the hill could sew. That is, everyone except me. Gladys's work was so fine that she could even make lace. Nearly everyone in town called upon her niece, Hatti, to make wedding dresses. My mother also had the gift, constructing magnificent costumes out of flashy fabrics for my sisters' skating competitions. But not me; I preferred cooking—using old wooden bowls, hand carved knives and choppers, maple spoons and Gladys's wood stove. While cooking or sewing or doing projects, the old folks told stories about whatever came to mind. When they came to a story I said I had not heard before (which happened less and less as I grew older), they would laugh and say, "Oh my, your

education has been sadly neglected," then proceed to tell the tale EXHAUS-
TIVELY.

A major event of my childhood occurred in 1967. Gladys, Harold,
Courtland Fowler (later Chief Little Hatchet), and a host of other elders took
my cousin David and me, along with our many other cousins, to attend
the opening of the Mohegan-Pequot Bridge. Chief Tantaquidgeon had insisted on that name for the bridge since it spanned the Thames River, thus
physically reuniting the Mohegans and Pequots. Our tribes had lived on
opposite sides for more than three hundred years, since the division of our
nation under Sachems Uncas and Sassacus. Harold and Courtland intro-

Opening of the Mohegan-Pequot Bridge, 1967. Chief Harold
Tantaquidgeon is cutting the ribbon with Governor Dempsey. The
children (at front from left) are Melissa Fawcett, David Fowler (with
headband), Bruce Fowler, and (behind) Loretta Fielding Schultz,
Gladys, and Courtland Fowler.

duced David and me to Governor John Dempsey and asked us to present him with copies of *Mohegan Chief: The Story of Harold Tantaquidgeon* and *Uncas: Sachem of the Wolf People,* both by Virginia Frances Voight. While we nearly froze that day, we sensed that great changes were about to happen at Mohegan, and that not all of them might be good.

I noticed some of those not-so-great changes in the 1970s. By the time I was about seventeen, home construction had ripped apart the Mohegan woodlands. That same year, I first showed serious interest in herbal cures, and Gladys took me into those much-depleted woods. We gathered what we could throughout the season, then pressed our plant samples between sheets of waxed paper and stapled them onto cardboard, adding annotations for museum exhibition. In truth, there was not much to exhibit. All we found was a little sumac, rattlesnake plantain, yarrow, mint, mullein, and boneset—not much else. My greatest lesson that summer was not in herbal medicine but in mourning the loss of so many childhood friends among the plant people of the Mohegan woodlands.

About that same time, Gladys made my first formal adult regalia, beaded with leaves from those rare herbs. Much like her own ceremonial dress, mine consisted of a blue satin shirt, black skirt, and red leggings with blue trim. My collar was made of black velvet, with red piping forming the Trail of Life, accented by beaded people-dots, representing starry and earthly forms. Four directional symbols appeared at the back and on either side of the neck, each punctuated by a red-beaded center circle—representing the spiritual life force of the universe. Now that I had learned the meaning of these symbols, Gladys finally allowed me to wear them.

For Mohegans, layers of history are woven into these symbols. Harold offered stories about other nations as a tool with which to pierce these deeper layers of understanding. His lesson linked Mohegan truths with those of other groups to create a seamless whole. Gladys's words on the subject were identical in purpose. She explained simply that "most people don't understand that all things are connected." Occasionally, she offered examples of that connection, such as: "Our people always knew that faraway comets signaled the coming of war here on earth." She viewed both celestial and earthly happenings as part of current events.

In 1978, I enrolled in Georgetown University's School of Foreign Service in Washington, D.C., to major in world history and international relations. After my freshman year, I came home to the hill for summer vacation, and Gladys dubbed me assistant curator at Tantaquidgeon Museum. I returned to Washington in September as an intern at the Smithsonian Institution photo archives—to increase my museum skills. That autumn the weather in Washington was toxic, there was sky-high humidity, and the trees turned a sickly drab color. Thanks to my cousin, Norma Smith, I survived those doldrums: she sent me brilliant red and yellow leaves from Mohegan Hill. As a little girl, Gladys had taught me why those leaves changed color. She said that every year the Great Hunter (Orion) captured the Sky Bear (Ursa Major) and roasted him until his blood and fat dripped onto the earth below, coloring the leaves.

After college, I wanted to be nearer home and applied for graduate studies in history at the University of Connecticut and Harvard in 1982. Harvard invited Gladys and me to meet with the head of the *anthropology* department. The highlight of our trip was that Gladys tried quiche for the first time at the faculty club. The low point was that the school's representative tried to divert me from history to anthropology.

Like Gladys fifty years before, I worried that I was a very desirable subject for anthropology but a far too controversial student of history. I insisted that the story of American Indian people and all indigenous nations was the crux of world history, and that academia could not segregate us into anthropology. After refusing to apply to the anthropology department, I received a formal rejection notice, along with a lengthy letter from the head of the history department explaining that Indians were not the subjects of real history and that Harvard did not consider ethnohistory a discipline—not in the early 1980s anyway.

After receiving my master's degree in history from the University of Connecticut, I was married in 1984. Gladys performed the wedding ceremony at Tantaquidgeon Museum, offering age-old prayers beneath a brush arbor of thanksgiving. Chief Little Hatchet told my mother that he saw the Little People that hot July day. She whispered that blessing to me, and we both fell silent in our gratitude.

Gladys had just retired from the Tribal Council that year and asked that I replace her as vice-chair. I held that post for three years, after which I resigned to devote time to my young children, Rachel Beth, Madeline Fielding, and David Uncas. I had named Rachel after Rachel Hoscott Fielding (Gladys's great-grandmother). Madeline's middle name came from Fidelia Fielding, Flying Bird, because our house filled with birds while I was expecting her. Then, as David was being born in 1991, I received a vision of my late uncle, Harold Tantaquidgeon, passing him to me along the Beautiful White Path. Thus, David was given the middle name of Harold's hero—Sachem Uncas.

When Montville celebrated its bicentennial in 1986, Gladys and I prepared an exhibit commemorating those two centuries of goodwill between the Mohegan Indians and the townspeople. The town, in turn, dedicated its yearbook to Gladys and Harold. Sachem Uncas had promised friendship with the non-Indians, and his descendants remained obligated by that commitment.

Ensuring good relations between the tribe and the colony (later the state) required Mohegans to honor Connecticut at every one of their special occasions. In turn, in 1986, the University of Connecticut created a scholarship in Gladys's name, and the following year, the state of Connecticut presented her with an honorary doctoral degree in humane causes. Long-lasting relationships, like the one between the Mohegans and Connecticut, are hard wrought, but they are an enduring bond.

Besides friendship with the non-Indian, another Mohegan requirement was "Do what your elders tell you." Until the 1990s, parochial spirits dominated Mohegan Hill. For instance, Gladys insisted that I never attend local powwows because illegitimate tribes often sponsored them; many of these events she deemed nothing more than "flea markets for wannabees." I disagreed, however, since powwows were still the best way to meet other Indians, but not until 1992 did she permit me to go to one for the first time.

This powwow issue was divisive at Mohegan in the early 1990s. Many still remembered the old-time Wigwam festivals as the "pure ceremonial form." The tribe decided to bridge the discord by calling our annual event the Mohegan Wigwam Pow Wow. After that, the Council of Elders voted to refer to it only as the Wigwam. Whatever it is called, the annual Wigwam is again a sturdy annual fixture at Mohegan.

Another major Mohegan prohibition, visiting the Sandy Desert, was reversed in the mid-1990s. That area had been off-limits to Mohegans since memory. After due consideration, Gladys agreed, first, to let me and others survey the area and, eventually, to rebuild our reservation there.

To regain that land, the tribe had to win federal recognition of its sovereign status. Although the process had begun in 1978, the pace picked up in 1992, when the tribe opened its first office, outfitted with Ruth's rickety used furniture and old lamps, across the street from Gladys's home. I became the first employee, serving as federal recognition coordinator, but I still helped out at Tantaquidgeon Museum if crowds suddenly appeared. Gladys continued to handle things pretty much on her own until her ninety-eighth year. By then, her ankles were no bigger around than a silver dollar, and they no longer held up to climbing the hill.

Meantime, I consulted with Gladys and Ruth constantly regarding tidbits of tribal history related to federal recognition criteria. When the tribe received federal status on March 7, 1994, Gladys decided that I needed a new regalia. Since her sewing was not what it used to be, she purchased a Delaware-style blouse and skirt for me to wear with the beaded collar and leggings she had made me in the seventies.

A year later, all tribal staff (which had grown to nearly fifty) traveled to Washington, D.C., to celebrate the Sandy Desert lands being placed in trust for the tribe. We toasted every ancestor we could think of in thanksgiving. Ruth Tantaquidgeon came too, on her very first airplane ride. On arriving back at the hill around midnight, Roberta Cooney, my mother, Jayne, my cousin David Fowler, Ruth, and I rang the bell at Mohegan Church. Roberta said, "This is the best day of my life," and we knew it was all right to wake up Gladys and all the other creatures of the hill on that special night.

The next morning, the ancestors called Loretta Roberge, Courtland Fowler, and me to meet at Shantok, where we conveyed the good news to them at their burying grounds. A walking red-tailed hawk greeted us, paused at several graves, then sat in a tree, while an eagle circled overhead. As we watched, we nodded, sharing the oldest language of all.

When construction at the reservation was nearly completed for the Mohegan Sun resort in 1996, Gladys agreed to travel there, a mile down the hill. Along with Anita Fowler, my mother, and me, she donned her first hard hat to tour the building's four quadrants, dedicated to each of the four directions. We pointed out where we had used the designs that she had passed on to us. We also pointed out elements of her own personal style as well—such as chairs made of cowhide and Navajo blankets, inspired by treasures at Tantaquidgeon Museum. Her comment was, "This is great—a little too much green—but I don't suppose there's anything we can do about that now." (Gladys has always taught that green is a bad luck color for Mohegans.) Since that was her only criticism, we were relieved. Ruth immediately noticed what we all had hoped would be readily apparent, that "Mohegan Sun's really a tribute to Gladys's life's work!"

Gladys had far from completed that life's work, however. In fact, at one hundred years of age she has yet to retire. From 1995 on, Gladys and Ruth worked closely with Anita Fowler and me on repatriation of artifacts under the Native American Graves Protection and Repatriation Act. Items returned in the late 1990s include Sachem Uncas's bowl, Samson Occum's elm bark box, Emma Baker's mortar and pestle, and hundreds of artifacts from Uncas's village at Shantok, as well as many human remains and funerary objects from the Royal Mohegan Burial Ground in Norwich. With the return of so many of our tribe's treasures, Gladys and Ruth told me that they had chosen a new Indian name for me. As a child, I had gone by Morning

Star, but the new name they gave me was Osowano—the flower on the corn plant.

When work began on the restoration of Mohegan Church in 1998, Ruth and Gladys monitored the tribal trucks going past their house on Church Lane. Forever focused on the activities of their people, they loved to quiz me and others about that project, which proceded under the careful guidance of David Fowler. Like many other Mohegan places and people, the church was making a long steady journey back from nearly being lost forever.

There on the hill, our Mohegan life trails have followed clear and thorny paths, through simple and not-so-simple days, on a combined journey home and to forever.

Ni ya yo mo. It is ever so.

NOTES

1. The Mohegan name has been spelled many different ways by the various European colonists who encountered the tribe. Chief Harold Tantaquidgeon (1904–1989) humorously attributed it to the fact that "the Indian didn't talk too good, and the white man didn't hear too good."
2. For information on the history of the Mohegan Tribe, see Melissa Jayne Fawcett, *The Lasting of the Mohegans* (Mohegan, Conn.: Mohegan Tribe, 1995).
3. The precise year of Uncas's passing has long been contended. However, Medicine Woman Emma Baker recorded the date in her private papers as 1683.
4. Gladys passed on the belief that remarkable people turn into stars by telling the following story: "Years ago, there were seven wise men among the Indians. . . . The Creator thought that it was no use to place them on earth, as they were being constantly bothered by earthly things, so he placed them in the heavens. There we see the seven stars [Pleiades] as they were placed there so long ago by the Creator." The full version of this story and others may be found in Gladys Tantaquidgeon, *Folk Medicine of the Delaware and Related Algonkian Indians* (Harrisburg: Pennsylvania Historical and Museum Commission, [1972], 1995).
5. Personal papers of Gladys Tantaquidgeon, Uncasville, Conn.
6. In the Mohegan language, the word *anu* means "grandmother" and *nanu* refers to "my grandmother." This spelling is from a new Mohegan orthography created by the tribe's linguist, Dr. Julian Granberry, in 1999. *Nonner* is the early-twentieth-century spelling of this word used by Frank G. Speck in "Native Tribes and Dialects of Connecticut," in *Forty-third Annual Report of the Bureau of American Ethnology* (Washington, D.C.: U.S. Government Printing Office, 1928). Despite Speck's spelling, however, there is no "r" sound in the word. It is pronounced "non' nuh."
7. Personal papers of Gladys Tantaquidgeon, Uncasville, Conn.
8. Speck, "Native Tribes and Dialects of Connecticut," 261.
9. This is a paraphrasing of Makiawisug rules taught to the author by Gladys.
10. Gladys Tantaquidgeon and Jayne G. Fawcett, "Symbolic Motifs on Painted Baskets of the Mohegan-Pequot," in *A Key into the Language of Woodsplint Baskets,* ed.

Ann McMullen and Russell G. Handsman (Washington, Conn.: Institute for American Indian Studies, 1987), 99–100.

11. Emma Baker statement, Mohegan Tribal Archives, Uncasville, Conn.

12. Tantaquidgeon papers.

13. This connection between mortars, pestles, corn, and Mohegan leadership is discussed in Russell G. Handsman, "Chahnameed and a Mohegan Woman's Mortars" and "Algonkian Women Resist Colonialism," and Melissa Fawcett Sayet, "Sociocultural Authority in Mohegan Society," all in *Artifacts* (Institute for American Indian Studies), Vol. 16, No. 3–4 (1988), 11–31.

14. J. D. Prince and Frank G. Speck, reprinted from "The Modern Pequots and Their Language," *American Anthropologist,* n.s. Vol. 6 (1904), 104–105.

15. Sympathy note from Clara Rogers, 1952, Tantaquidgeon papers.

16. The contemporary translation of *powwow* comes from the Narragansett Medicine Woman Ella Sekatau and the Narragansett Tribal Historic Preservation Officer John B. Brown III.

17. Jeanette Fielding, "Welcome to the Wigwam," 1910, mimeographed copy in Mohegan Tribal Archives, Uncasville.

18. Nettie Fowler statement, n.d., Mohegan Tribal Archives.

19. Speck, "Native Tribes and Dialects of Connecticut," 225. In *The Life and Times of Frank G. Speck, 1881–1950* (Philadelphia: University of Pennsylvania Publications in Anthropology No. 4, 1991), 1, Roy Blankenship claims that "at the age of eight, Frank went to live with Mrs. Fidelia Fielding, a friend of the family, at Mohegan, Connecticut. . . . here Frank remained until about age fifteen." Gladys states that this account is pure fantasy; Speck did not meet Fidelia until he was a Columbia University student conducting Mohegan ethnography.

20. Gladys Tantaquidgeon, "Notes on the Gay Head Indians of Massachusetts," *Indian Notes* (New York: Museum of the American Indian, Heye Foundation), Vol. 7, No. 1 (January, 1930), 24–26.

21. Roger Williams, *A Key into the Language of America* (London: Gregory Dexter, 1643), 110.

22. Tantaquidgeon papers.

23. Ibid.

24. Ibid.

25. This information recorded from official brochures of the Oglala Indians and the accounts of Loretta Roberge, Corresponding Secretary of the Mohegan Tribal

Council, following a 1998 council visit to the Oglala Lakota Nation, Mohegan Tribal Archives.

26. John W. De Forest, *History of the Indians of Connecticut from the Earliest Known Period to 1850* (Hartford, Conn.: W. J. Hammersley, 1851).

27. *Christian Science Monitor,* Sept. 5, 1936, copy in Tantaquidgeon papers.

28. Press release, March 1, 1938, ibid.

29. *Mademoiselle,* October 1947, page number not given, copy in Tantaquidgeon papers.

30. Tantaquidgeon papers.

31. Gladys's *Folk Medicine of the Delaware and Related Algonkian Indians* first appeared as *A Study of Delaware Indian Medicine Practice and Folk Beliefs* (Harrisburg: Pennsylvania Historical Commission, 1942).

32. Gladys quoted in Melissa Fawcett, *The Lasting of the Mohegans.* An excellent biography of Harold Tantaquidgeon is Virginia Frances Voight, *Mohegan Chief: The Story of Harold Tantaquidgeon* (New York: Funk and Wagnalls, 1965).

33. Jayne Fawcett's speech has been reprinted several times. See, for example, Norwich (Conn.) *Bulletin,* Jan. 7, 1996, B2–B3. After 1769, the Connecticut colony no longer fully acknowledged the Mohegan sachemdom. See John de Forest, *History of the Indians of Connecticut,* 460–63.

34. Norwich *Bulletin,* June 25, 1994, editorial page.

35. Sam Gejdenson's letter is in the Mohegan Tribal Archives. It was quoted in Nancy Trimble, "Celebration Honors Mohegan Medicine Woman Gladys Tantaquidgeon's 100th Birthday," *Ni Ya Yo* (Uncasville, Conn.), Vol. 1, No. 11 (1999), 3. All the other unattributed quotations in this chapter come from the author's notes taken on that occasion.

BIBLIOGRAPHY

Fawcett, Melissa Jayne. *The Lasting of the Mohegans*. Mohegan, Conn.: Mohegan Tribe, 1995.

Mohegan Tribal Archives, Uncasville, Conn.

Prince, J. D., and Frank G. Speck. Special limited edition booklet reprinted from "The Modern Pequots and Their Language." *American Anthropologist* n.s. 6:1. (January–March 1904).

Speck, Frank G. "Native Tribes and Dialects of Connecticut." In *Forty-third Annual Report of the Bureau of American Ethnology*. Washington, D.C.: U.S. Government Printing Office, 1928.

Tantaquidgeon, Gladys. Personal papers. Uncasville, Conn.

———. *Folk Medicine of the Delaware and Related Algonkian Indians*. Harrisburg: Pennsylvania Historical and Museum Commission, [1972], 1995.

———. "Notes on the Gay Head Indians of Massachusetts." *Indian Notes* 7:1. New York: Museum of the American Indian, Heye Foundation, January 1930.

Tantaquidgeon, Gladys, and Jayne G. Fawcett. "Symbolic Motifs on Painted Baskets of the Mohegan-Pequot." In *A Key into the Language of Woodsplint Baskets*. Ed. Ann McMullen and Russell G. Handsman. Washington, Conn.: Institute for American Indian Studies, 1987.

Trimble, Nancy. "Celebration Honors Mohegan Medicine Woman Gladys Tantaquidgeon's 100th Birthday." *Ni Ya Yo* (Uncasville, Conn.) 1:11 (1999).

Voight, Virginia Frances. *Mohegan Chief: The Story of Harold Tantaquidgeon*. New York: Funk and Wagnalls, 1965.

ABOUT THE AUTHOR

Melissa Jayne Fawcett is the tribal historian for the Mohegan
Indian Nation in Connecticut. She also serves as Executive
Director of the Mohegan Tribal Museum Authority. Her great-
aunt, Medicine Woman Dr. Gladys Tantaquidgeon, trained her
in tribal oral tradition, traditional lifeways, and spiritual
beliefs. Since childhood she has worked with Gladys at the
Tantaquidgeon Museum. After receiving a B.S.F.S. in history
and diplomacy from Georgetown University and an M.A. in
history from the University of Connecticut, she traveled
throughout New England as a storyteller for the tribe. In 1992
she received the North American Native Writers' First Book
Award in Creative Nonfiction from the Native Writers' Circle
of the Americas for *The Lasting of the Mohegans*. Beginning in
1992, Fawcett served as federal recognition coordinator for the
Mohegans, and the tribe successfully attained federal recognition on March 7, 1994. That same year Fawcett became the first
American Indian appointed by the governor to the Connecticut Historical Commission. Two years later she received the
first annual Chief Little Hatchet Award (the tribe's highest
honor), granted for contributions to the success and survival
of the Mohegan people. Fawcett's previous publications
include a traditional Mohegan children's story coauthored
with Joseph Bruchac and entitled *Makiawisug: The Gift of the
Little People*. She lives on Mohegan Hill with her three children, Rachel, Madeline, and David Uncas.